101 KNIFE DESIGNS

PRACTICAL KNIVES FOR DAILY USE

MURRAY CARTER

Published by

Krause Publications a division of F+W Media, Inc.
700 East State Street • Iola, WI 54990-0001
715-445-2214 • 888-457-2873
www.krausebooks.com

To order books or other products call toll-free 1-800-258-0929
or visit us online at www.shopblade.com

Cover photography by Kris Kandler
Photography by Hiro Soga

ISBN-13: 978-1-4402-3383-8
ISBN-10: 1-4402-3383-7

Cover Design by Dustin Reid
Designed by Dave Hauser
Illustrations by Megan Merkel
Edited by Corrina Peterson

Printed in the United States of America

10 9 8 7 6

[TABLE OF CONTENTS]

[ACKNOWLEDGEMENTS]

MY FRIEND, FELLOW ABS MASTER BLADESMITH ED FOWLER ONCE WROTE "THERE'S NOTHING EASY ABOUT MAKING KNIVES FOR A LIVING." THEREFORE, I WOULD LIKE TO DEDICATE THIS BOOK TO ALL THE HARD-WORKING KNIFEMAKERS IN THE WORLD, CURRENT AND FUTURE, WHO WILL KEEP HANDMADE KNIVES POURING FORTH IN THE YEARS TO COME FOR THE WHOLE WORLD'S BENEFIT. I WOULD ALSO LIKE TO DEDICATE THIS WORK TO THE GRACIOUS PATRONS WHO DO AND WILL BUY THOSE KNIVES, AND MORE IMPORTANTLY, ENCOURAGE AND SUPPORT THE BLADE MAKERS OF TODAY AND TOMORROW.

[DISCLAIMER]

This book is all about practical knife designs. It is written for the reader who desires first and foremost to make or own a knife that will be held and used for extended periods of time to cut things. This doesn't mean to imply that other types of blades and knives, such as Fantasy or Art knives, have no merit in the cutlery world. Definitely not! Fantasy and Art knives offer richness and variety to the cutlery market, for everyone's benefit. As these knives are limited only by the artist's imagination and skills, it is exciting to see what will come along next in this exciting arena of knife design.

At the end of the day however, it is the practical knives that will get continual use for meaningful tasks and will become cherished keepsakes of their owners. I believe it is imperative that any aspiring full-time knifemaker offer several practical knives in their repertoire. While it is possible for a select gifted few to make a good living selling only fantasy or art knives, most other knifemakers will survive periods of tough economic times by offering some knives that customers can actually use.

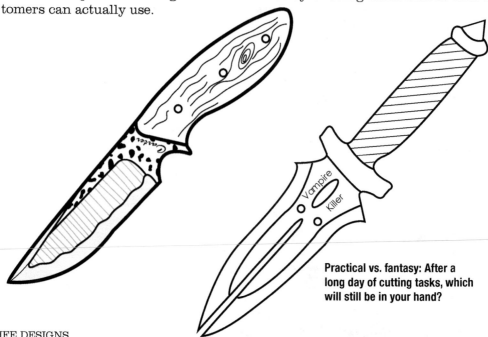

Practical vs. fantasy: After a long day of cutting tasks, which will still be in your hand?

A note on the distinction between the terms blade, handle and knife, and how the terms length, width and thickness apply.

I define a **blade** as being the part of a knife that slices, chops or pierces as measured from the furthest tip to the beginning of the handle. If a knife has a guard or bolster, that is where the blade begins. If a knife has no guard, the blade begins at the front of the material that constitutes the handle.

The **handle** is the part of the knife that is held in the hand during regular use. The handle includes the metal guard if the knife has one. The end of the handle is the part of the knife furthest away from the blade tip. A knife is defined as a blade with a handle so as to be held in the hand during use.

The term **length** when referring to the blade means the dimensions of the blade from tip to the start of the handle. (However, kitchen knife blade length is measured from the heel of the blade to the tip).

Width is the dimension from the spine of the blade to the cutting edge (or cutting edge to cutting edge in the case of a dagger). The terms wide and narrow are used to describe width.

Thickness is the dimension of the fattest part of the blade between the right and left sides. Thickness will always be a smaller dimension than width. Thin, light, thick and heavy are terms used to describe a blade's thickness.

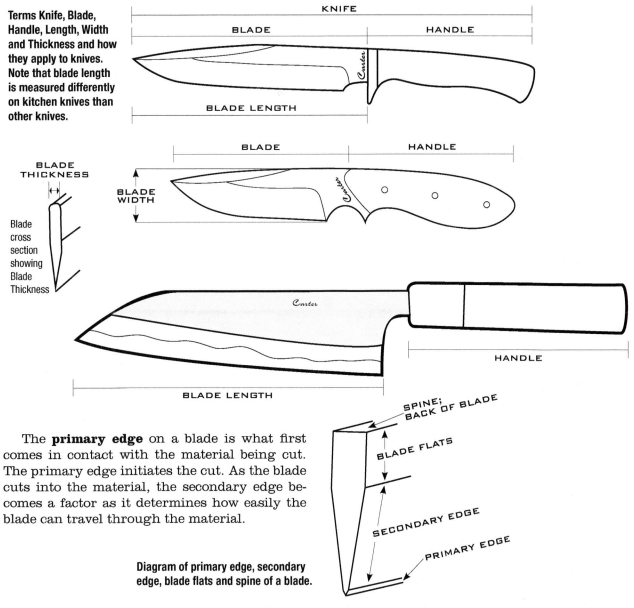

Terms Knife, Blade, Handle, Length, Width and Thickness and how they apply to knives. Note that blade length is measured differently on kitchen knives than other knives.

Blade cross section showing Blade Thickness

The **primary edge** on a blade is what first comes in contact with the material being cut. The primary edge initiates the cut. As the blade cuts into the material, the secondary edge becomes a factor as it determines how easily the blade can travel through the material.

Diagram of primary edge, secondary edge, blade flats and spine of a blade.

Named after my old forge in Japan where I first made this pattern, the Tabaruzaka Utility neck knife is as slick as they come. It features a Hitachi white steel #1/stainless laminate blade, HRC 64, unpolished hammer forged finish and a reverse "coffee jelly" handle (brown and black micarta).

INTRODUCTION

Like many North American boys, I have been fascinated with knives and things that go "cut" since my early childhood. As fate would have it, I ended up in Japan at the age of 18 where I fell into an apprenticeship with a 16th generation Yoshimoto bladesmith that lasted six years. Upon completion of that fortunate tutelage, I continued forging blades in Japan for twelve more years, moved to the U.S. in 2005 and have continued forging blades since then. To date I have personally completed over 17,000 knives, the majority of which were one-of-a-kind pieces consistent with the kind of work done by old-world artisans.

I am indeed very fortunate to have found paying customers for most of those knives. As it was in the early days of my career, so it remains today a challenge to create knives that are appealing enough for customers to feel the compulsion to part with their hard-earned cash to buy one of my premium blades. I do believe that I have learned a thing or two during that time about appealing knife design. Teaching others at my exclusive Traditional Japanese Bladesmithing School has further refined my convictions on the topic. It has been a double blessing in helping me communicate both the obvious

(above) Hand sharpening a combat knife at the Tabaruzaka Forge, Kumamoto, Japan, 2002.

(left) Carter Family in front of the Tabaruzaka Forge in 2001.

(below) 17th Generation Yoshimoto Bladesmith Murray Carter. Who will be the 18th?

and also the subtleties of the lines of knives.

I invite you now to join with me as I explore the successful common traits in popular knife design that have lasted throughout all of man's history. Both enthusiast and maker alike will learn how to identify the common traits in great knives, and the latter will better understand how to apply them to new knife design.

It can be said that knives are task-specific tools with only three objectives: to slice, chop or pierce.

Slicing is moving a relatively thin blade through

(right) Almost all the way through a stiff Japanese coffee can. These cans are as thick as the old apple juice cans from the 1970s.

(below) Pioneering research of a blade's ability to cut through empty steel cans. This was before it became a popular test in North American cutting competitions.

Author at a Japanese craft show in 2000, set up with his travelling forge. Local kids came to get a free lesson on basic forging techniques. In view is the wheel-well forge with coke fire, hand-made leather bellows and Peddinghous anvil which is still the center piece of Murray's shop today. When Murray ordered that anvil from Wisconsin in the late 90s, they air-freighted it to Japan at a cost of over $2000! In the background is Murray's faithful bike, a Honda CRM 250, on which he put over 50,000 miles.

the subject matter in a perpendicular fore or aft drawing motion. A relatively long section of the blade comes into contact with the same area of the subject matter as the blade is drawn through perpendicularly. The doctor's use of a scalpel during surgery or removal of a thin slice of beef from a roast are two examples of slicing.

Chopping is contacting one isolated part of a blade directly with enough force to cleave though the subject matter. There is no fore/aft motion as in slicing. To withstand the great forces involved, chopping blades must be stout and necessarily thicker than slicing blades. Removing small limbs from a tree or removing the head from a fish are examples of chopping.

Slicing the fat from beef using a Carter Whitecrane.

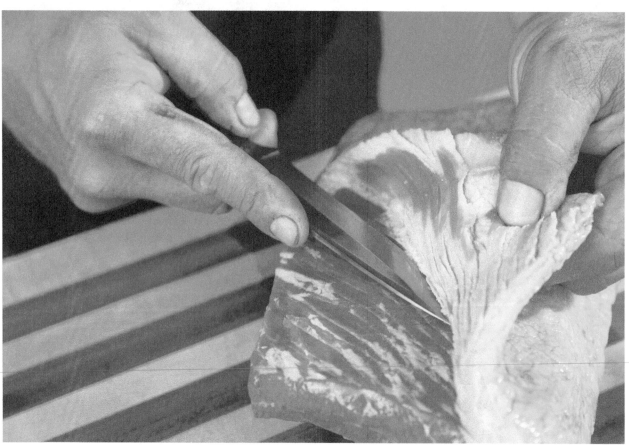

Chopping wood with a Japanese laminated axe.

(above) Author uses his EDC neck knife for almost everything.
Beware of the person with one knife!

(right) Chamfers on back of blade enable low drag piercing.

Piercing is inserting the blade from the point directly into the subject matter in a straight line. Stabbing an olive with a toothpick or skewering meat for a shish-kebob are examples of piercing.

A blade can be either single purposed or, more commonly, a combination of two or more of these objectives. Generally speaking, the more task specific the design, the more efficient it will be at performing tasks for which it was designed. Conversely, the blades designed to do all, i.e., pierce, slice and chop, do none of these individual tasks with absolute efficiency.

Think of how adept the axe is at chopping, but lacking acute edge geometry, is ill-suited to slice and has no point to pierce. Likewise the skinning knife excels at slicing, but lacking the mass to chop well or an in-line point to pierce. The dagger excels at piercing, but lacks edge geometry or curvature to slice or chop.

One of my goals then is to illuminate design features in blades that aid the knife in accomplishing each of these tasks perfectly or a com-

bination of these tasks with the least compromise possible.

Another concept that I explore is how our subconscious evaluation of knives stems from prehistoric times when man first started to use tools. Not born with any deadly teeth or claws, man had to utilize what he saw and found for both defense and also to carve out for himself a niche in the wilderness. Man's first sharp tools and weapons were scavenged teeth, bones, horns and stones.

"Thus man, essentially a tool-making animal, and compelled by the conditions of his being to one long battle with the brute creation, was furnished by his enemies, not only with models of implements and instruments, and with instructions to use them, from witnessing the combats of brutes, but actually with their arms, which he converted to his own purpose." – Richard F. Burton, *The Book of The Sword*

In his excellent book dating back over one hundred years ago, Richard Burton argues that man's first exploitation of natural weapons was using teeth and horns from animals. Careful observation of how the animals used their teeth and horns taught man the most efficient use of the curved, pointy teeth and long horns for slicing, chopping and piercing. Before man ever discovered bronze or steel, he had perfected the necessary arm thrusts, jabs and slashes that resulted in deadly blows with his weapons and constructive cuts with his tools.

When referring to various weapons made from animals teeth and horns, Burton comments, "Here we see the association in the maker's mind between the animal from which the weapon is derived and the purpose of destruction for which it is chiefly used." That is to say, early man watched horned animals lunge and poke at each other, and he concluded that straight pointy objects were good for the same purpose in his hands. Likewise, he saw the beasts use sharp teeth and claws to great effect in slicing and chopping and then endeavored to procure and use them in the same manner.

Since those days when man first started to use the animal horns, bones, teeth, claws and stones around him, he started to develop an eye for 'seeing' the potential in the natural resources in terms of effectiveness in slicing, chopping and piercing. Discretion quickly developed to discern between one oddly shaped, structurally weak horn and a straight, narrow and strong horn which was better for piercing. At a glance, our ancestors could distinguish the finest tooth among a set of teeth belonging to a fallen animal he stumbled upon. He wouldn't pick up the pearly one or the most unusual, but rather the one he knew would serve him the best as a slicing/chopping/piercing tool. If he chose the wrong one, he would suffer later for his bad choice in terms of extra effort and labor required to use the tool. Survival was a strong motivation and a merciless teacher in superior

Author with his wife at a knife show in Aso, Kumamoto, Japan. Oct. 2000. It is amazing to watch patrons consistently pick up the same knife first when they visit my table. Notice the cleanly cut coffee can on the edge of the table…proof that Murray's can cutting research predated similar activities later conducted in North America.

blade design.

It is my argument that when we see a truly well designed knife, our subconscious, molded by millennia of tool using, recognizes it as being a superior tool. So many times have I been at knife expositions with at least thirty knives on the table, only to have 99% of the visitors initially pick up the same knife to look at. This 99% figure is not only made up of enthusiastic men, but includes children, wives and grandmothers as well. I have witnessed this phenomenon at almost every knife show I have attended. This tends to happen to other knifemakers as well, to the best of my observation. What is especially interesting is that the popular knife is usually not the one with the fanciest handle or the outlandish design, but rather the one which the examiner could most readily identify as being well suited to efficiently slice, chop or pierce.

Tetsuo model neck knife named after the author's son. Tetsuo means "Ironman." This one has an ironwood handle, naturally!

Carter Cutlery patrons visit with Murray at the Oregon Knife Collector's Show in Eugene Oregon, April, 2008.

The eyes have sized up every knife in view and the subconscious has made a judgment as to the best tool on the table.

Another very interesting observation is what the visitors do when they pick up the knife and position it in their hand. They make small slicing, chopping or piercing motions, as if to confirm with the physical senses what the subconscious has already decided. In silence and with a barely imperceptible nod of the head the visitor feels the efficiency of the blade as it slices, chops and pierces objects only visible to them. Their senses and mind fully convinced that they have discovered a "winner" they often reverentially set the knife back on the table with the quiet utterance "THAT is a nice knife!" If their finances allow, they will usually buy the knife on the spot.

So what is it that makes that knife so special? What are the design features that work so powerfully on the subconscious? I believe there are a few simple features that explain why certain blade designs have stood the test of time and remain popular. Practical blade patterns follow several rules of thumb, and when these rules are applied to new knife designs by blade makers, there is a greater chance the design will be accepted by the public, and more importantly, stand the test of time. Follow along as we examine distinctive features in slicing, chopping

Close up of the blade of the Tetsuo model necker. This one is stamped "Rudy" on the reverse side and was made for our expert firearms instructor who is featured in our Combat Handgun High Performance Tips on YouTube.

Museum Specimens and Those That Didn't Make It

Some claim that the best way to study successful blade designs of antiquity is to frequent museums and historical sites. These places usually sport a healthy collection of blades and tools from the past. However, the blades available for study can't speak for the other blades, the contemporaries of their time, that are not available for observation. I am chiefly speaking of the blades that were so well favored by their owners that they got continually used, continually sharpened, until they were worn away to practically nothing. These blades never made it to the museum, primarily because they were the best blades the owners had and therefore they got used up. Conversely, just like in our age, those knives that just don't feel right in the hand, or the ones that can't perform their intended task very well, are left sitting, collecting dust while the "favorite" knife is continually put to work. It is therefore my assertion that not many high quality (well designed and with good metallurgy) blades ever made it to the museum. Those tools and blades we see in such venues are mostly those which were rejected for some reason or another. Perhaps it was due to the blade design, the handle design, poor metallurgy or a combination thereof.

In Japan, it is commonly said that one will rarely find a good carpenter's tool in a second-hand store. The good tools were used up. The less useful were "recycled."

We must then, be cautious about drawing conclusions about the effectiveness of the designs from knives we encounter from the past. Generally speaking, the more pristine the condition of an antique blade, the more we need to suspect its credentials. If the blade looks like it was heavily used at some time, then we can assume it has some positive attributes.

Does anyone really wonder why this one made it to the museum?

and/or piercing knives that were equally popular from man's early time to today.

Ideal Blade Shapes for Slicing, Chopping and Piercing, with Historical Examples

Slicing blades were made from knapping various stones, such as flint and obsidian, as well as teeth from animals. These blades were severely limited by their small size. Better, long thin curved slicing knives didn't come about until the discovery of bronze. The common trait of slicing knives is a very thin edge geometry and generous curvature of the cutting edge. The ideal slicing knife would be as thin as the material structure would allow and long enough to allow maximum slicing with one direction of movement. The blade would be as narrow as possible to reduce friction in the cut as the blade was moving through the material. Most slicing knives are wider than needed for superior slicing to allow for repeated sharpenings and longevity.

Chopping tools are amongst the earliest blade tools known to man. Thick, axe-like stones were used to separate flesh from animals and other tasks by holding the whole tool in the hand and pounding. Even with the discovery of metal, the shape of these hand choppers didn't change much initially, being cast out of pure copper, and later bronze, into objects looking very similar to our current axe heads. Momentum is the principle force at work with choppers, so these tools were thick and heavy. By the same token, momentum could also cause the edge to fail during cutting, so edge geometry was thick to withstand the blows. The ideal chopper would be heavy enough to supply the momentum required to cleave through the subject material, without being any thicker than absolutely necessary to withstand repeated use. Most chopping knives available today are thicker and heavier than they should be because manufacturers design them with the lowest common denominator in mind. They fear a blade being returned because it chipped during use, so they make them able to withstand the worst abuse imaginable.

Piercing tools, such as those horns and teeth that early man first saw employed by the brutes around him, are typically long, straight and thin. Sharpened sticks hardened by fire were also used. Coming from nature, these piercing tools were fairly blunt, which

Sketch of ancient Roman bronze slicing knife, circa 10 AD, excavated in France.

Author's "ideal" slicing knife. Note the resemblance to a Japanese katana.

From page 72, Book of the Sword, Richard F. Burton. Copper celts in the Dublin Collection.

required enormous force to penetrate the subject matter. Piercing weapons were often used for hunting or self-defense. In such cases, without the ability to cut as they were penetrating, major blood vessels and vital organs could be pushed out of the way by the weapon on entry, often resulting in a less-than-desirable strike.

It was the discovery of metal that enabled these blades to excel at piercing. Long, strong edged daggers and stilettos, perfected between the 13th and 15th century, embodied the very finest attributes of the piercing blade. The ideal piercing blade has a point of exceptional sharpness, in a straight line with the handle and in the natural direction of the thrust. The shape requires minimum effort to puncture the subject material, it is strong enough not to break when stressed, and it has razor sharp blades to slice surrounding material on entry.

One common feature of man's earliest piercing weapons was that they were narrow in cross-section near the tip, then progressively grew thicker and wider with length, such as a horn or tusk. This wedge-shaped cross-section required additional force to penetrate material with each millimeter of entry. A giant leap in efficiency was made when piercing weapons were shaped so that the length of the weapon was the same dimension as near the tip. Further refinement came about when piercing weapons were made to be thickest just behind the tip and then slightly narrower in cross section towards the hilt. This design produced less friction as the weapon entered flesh than one whose blade was the same width lengthwise. The Roman gladius and the African Massai warrior's spear come immediately to mind. A more recent successful blade design with this "leaf-like" blade shape is the Gerber MKII dagger, which was highly coveted by soldiers in Vietnam.

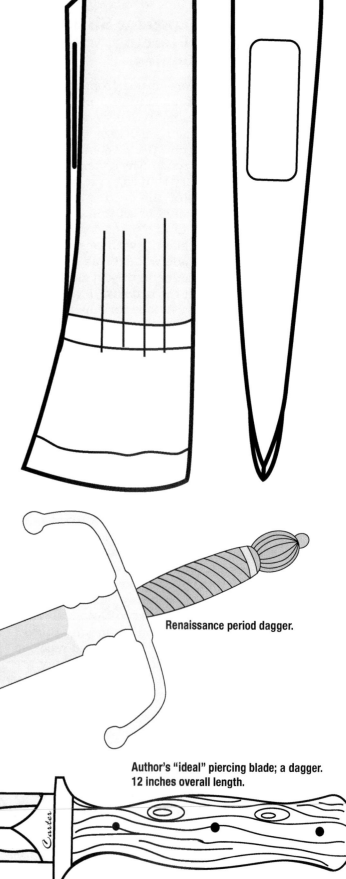

Author's "ideal" chopping blade…a Japanese Tosa axe!

Renaissance period dagger.

Author's "ideal" piercing blade; a dagger. 12 inches overall length.

Carter

Why Slicing in Only One Direction is Most Efficient

Many travelers to Japan (and YouTube junkies!) have observed in wonder as a Japanese fish monger or Sushi chef prepared and sliced jewels of the sea with long slender blades that looked far longer than necessary to the observers. These blades are in keeping with the Japanese knife philosophy that states slicing cuts should be made in only one direction and be one smooth continuous cut through to completion. This cutting philosophy results in slicing cuts that reduce cell damage to the fish and reduces the time required to make each cut.

Conversely, using shorter blades requires the blade to be used in a fore/aft sawing motion, or multiple passes in the same direction with lost time and precision as the blade is returned to the same starting point and repositioned in the progressive cut.

In the sawing motion example, as the blade is reversed in direction, inefficiencies include: 1) blade momentum must be arrested and then reversed, 2) as the blade direction is reversed, in the first few millimeters no material is being cut as the material sways slightly with the change in blade direction, and 3) massive cell damage occurs when the blade produces friction in one direction and then in the opposite direction, much like the crushing effect in wringing out a towel.

It is no surprise that the Japanese have mastered serving raw fresh fish to discerning food enthusiasts; they take the precautions necessary to prevent the oxidation (rotting) of cells in the fish meat that results from poor slicing techniques.

Fishmongers at the world's largest and most famous fish market, Tsukiji in Tokyo, Japan, use a very long "Maguro bocho" to slice up fresh tuna.

The Bladesmith's Paradox

Blade Thickness and Edge Geometry, including the Perfect Geometry of a Kitchen Knife

When asked what the best edge geometry for kitchen knives is, author simply responds with, "Thin!"

"Hai Sensei, usuku tsukurimashita! Ikaga deshou?!"

There is one fundamental aspect of blade making that hasn't changed or improved since the beginning of the trade. That is the dilemma of how thick and strong to make a blade. Simply put, a thicker blade will withstand greater adverse forces acting upon it, but at a direct sacrifice in cutting performance. The ultra-thin blades will slice like no other, but might fail when subject to heavy duty chores.

One approach to this problem is to "play it safe" by finishing the blade a little on the thick side, so that it will withstand repeated abuse. If a customer wants to, they can grind down the blade themselves for better cutting performance. The opposite approach, taken by traditional Japanese bladesmiths, is to err on the thin side, thereby producing a superior performing blade in terms of cutting.

As I write this essay, I can still hear my Sensei yelling at me when I was forging Japanese kitchen knives in my early days, "Motto usuku, MOTTO USUKU! Kauboi naifu tsukutteru-n JA NAI!" He was telling me in his own endearing way that I should be forging the blades as thin as I could. His gentle reminder was that I was forging a Japanese kitchen knife, and not a crow-bar! Something else he said that sticks with me is that blades always look thinner than they really are when you are forging them. Nowadays when I am forging, I go for "paper-thin" and they come out just about right.

If a thin blade is abused and the edge chips, the blade can simply be ground back at a slightly steeper angle to remove the chip. The resulting thicker edge geometry will resist chipping again under the same abuse. It is a system that reaches natural equilibrium in just a short time between the owner and blade.

Having forged and completed over 10,000 kitchen knives so far, I am often asked about the "perfect" kitchen knife geometry. My answer must seem ambiguous, but I just make them thin so that the owner can discover the "perfect geometry" as he uses and sharpens them back.

Pizza Cutter or Chopping Tool?

Pop-Quiz: What kind of blade is a rolling wheel pizza cutter? Although the motion to cut a pizza is a fore and aft motion with the hand, similar to slicing, the blade is, in fact, not slicing. Remember that slicing is defined as "a relatively thin blade moving through the subject matter in a perpendicular fore/aft drawing motion." A relatively long section of the blade comes into contact with the same area of the subject matter as the blade is drawn through.

If the pizza cutter wheel could spin of its own accord, and then was held in one place in order to cut the pizza, the blade action would be slicing, as a long part of the blade would come into contact with one isolated part of the pizza. However, such is not the case. Pizza cutters push their way through the pizza with a great force exerted; they act like chopping blades. The action is no different than if you placed the cutting edge of a long bladed knife perpendicular to the pizza and then pushed down on the spine of the knife with your support hand (which is exactly how the "other" pizza cutter, the mezzaluna, works). Therefore, the wheel pizza cutter is really a chopper. I'm guessing everyone will raise an eyebrow though, if you request "a chop of pizza, please."

This is close to what I see when I am examining a blade for perfect profiles. Notice how pointy the tip is, and this is before the final hand-sharpening I do before delivery to a customer.

APPLYING THE PRINCIPLES of practical knife design requires more than understanding; it also requires an eye for fine detail. Careful observation reveals fine scratches in the riveted pins on this skinning knife.

SLICING/PIERCING HYBRID: Ample secondary edge geometry and a graceful curving primary edge make for a good slicing knife in a compact, portable package. A point that lines up close to the center of the blade and handle give this knife some piercing ability as well.

From big to small, outdoor knives have "cool-factor."

PART ONE

DESIGN THEORY AND PRACTICAL DESIGNS FOR DAILY USE

While outdoor knives are the hands-down winner for their "cool-factor," the truth of the matter is that, when considering actual use, they play second fiddle to a group of knives that get used exponentially more, namely, kitchen knives. Let's first examine culinary blades and then turn our attention to hobby and outdoor knives.

When we are evaluating knives, we must ask ourselves, "What is this knife for?" Then we can assess its design merit in terms of how it slices, chops or pierces.

Culinary Blades

The knives that have seen the most daily use throughout the generations are undoubtedly those related to food preparation. Day in and day out, folks need to eat. The majority of kitchen knives are simple in design and efficient in use. They can be broken down into three categories: paring knives, slicing knives and chopping knives. Traditionally, a sharply-pointed slicing knife would also be used to slaughter animals, but is less common today.

I mentioned in my first book, Bladesmithing with Murray Carter (page 26 "The Magic of a Millimeter" and page 87 "Grinding a Perfect Blade Profile"), that, unlike outdoor knives which are primarily judged for their looks, kitchen knives are judged and purchased largely for their reputation as fine food preparation tools. A millimeter here or there in the design won't spoil a good kitchen knife as fast as poor metallurgy will. That said, well-designed kitchen knives share these common traits:

• Easy-to-sharpen blades with smooth flowing curves.

• An absence of serrations or recurve edge profiles.

• Blades that are as thin as possible, but strong enough for repeated use.

• Blades that are wider than needed to allow for years of constant sharpening.

• Blades for use in conjunction with the knuckles of the fingers as a cutting guide are wide, and can also be used to transport cut food

• Simple profile handles that are longer than the hand is wide, to allow for a variety of holding positions.

• Handles that do not get in the way of easily sharpening the blades.

• Simple to clean; absence of nooks and crannies where food particles could accumulate and rot.

International Pro Series Gyuto
in ironwood and brass.

Paring Knives

Small, thin-bladed knives (usually less than a 4-inch blade) are called paring knives. To pare means to remove the skin (or a layer) from a fruit or vegetable. When used in the hands, as when peeling a potato, the blade is actually chopping, insomuch as the edge is pushed straight through the material without any fore/aft slicing motion.

Paring knives are also used in conjunction with a cutting board to slice food using the forward portion of the blade. The rearward portion of the blade is rarely effective for slicing on a board, as the handle shape prevents using it this way.

Most paring knives have a sharpened point for occasional piercing tasks, such as opening food packaging and removing the core of a tomato.

A well designed paring knife has a simple blade with a nice simple, well rounded handle. The simple handle plays an extremely important role, as it allows tremendous flexibility in how the knife is gripped. When a knife can be held in the hand many different ways to accomplish many different cutting tasks, familiarity with the knife will quickly lead to mastery in its use. This may explain why most violent blade crimes are committed with kitchen cutlery...the intimately familiar blade will always make for the most effective weapon.

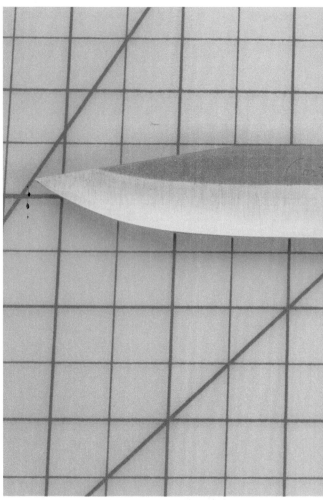

Kuro-uchi International Pro Series paring knife with corian handle and brass hardware. This knife would have benefitted by chamfering the top clip point for easier piercing, and more careful fitting of the brass guard.

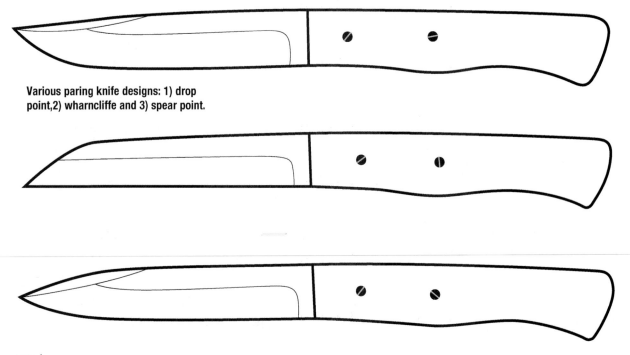

Various paring knife designs: 1) drop point, 2) wharncliffe and 3) spear point.

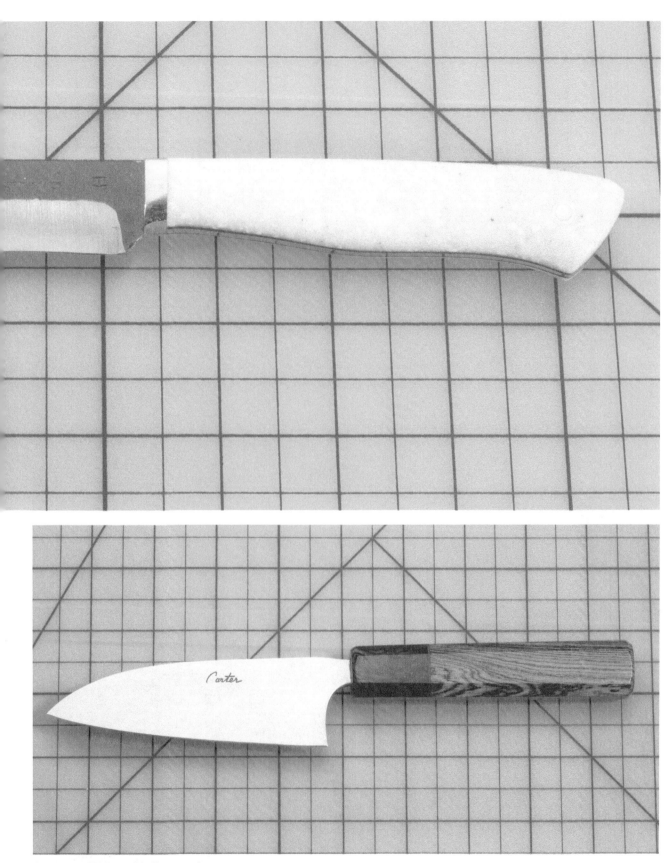

Japanese wide "petty" knife, sometimes used as a paring knife in Japanese cuisine. This one has a three layer laminate blade and a bocote/ironwood octagonal handle.

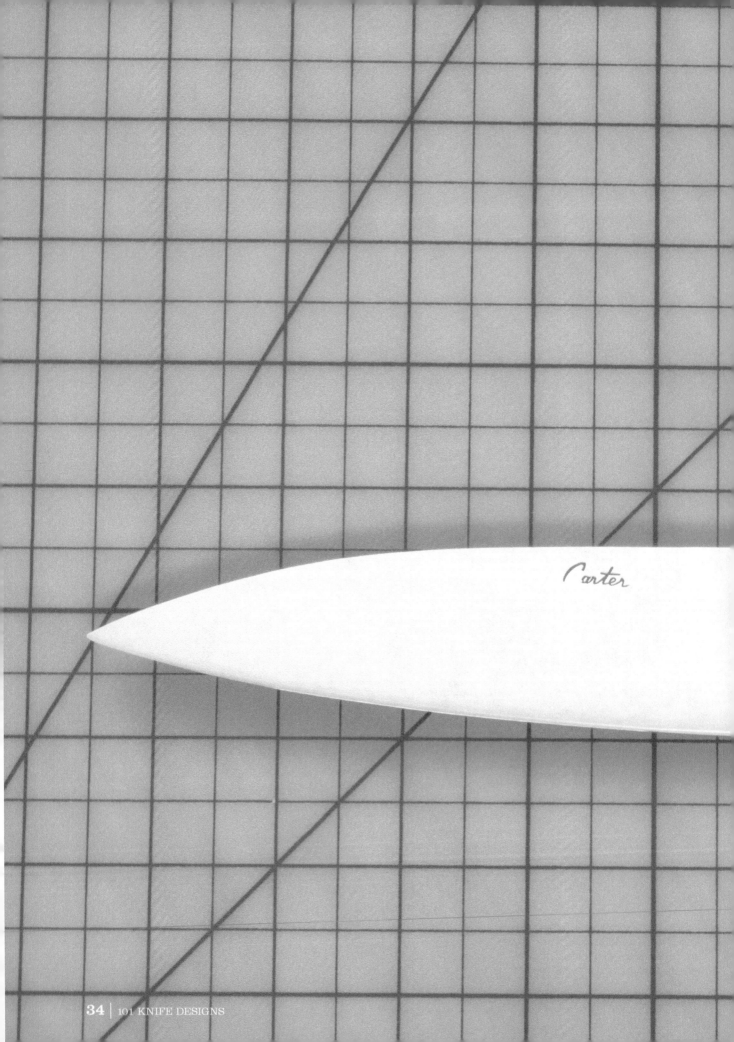

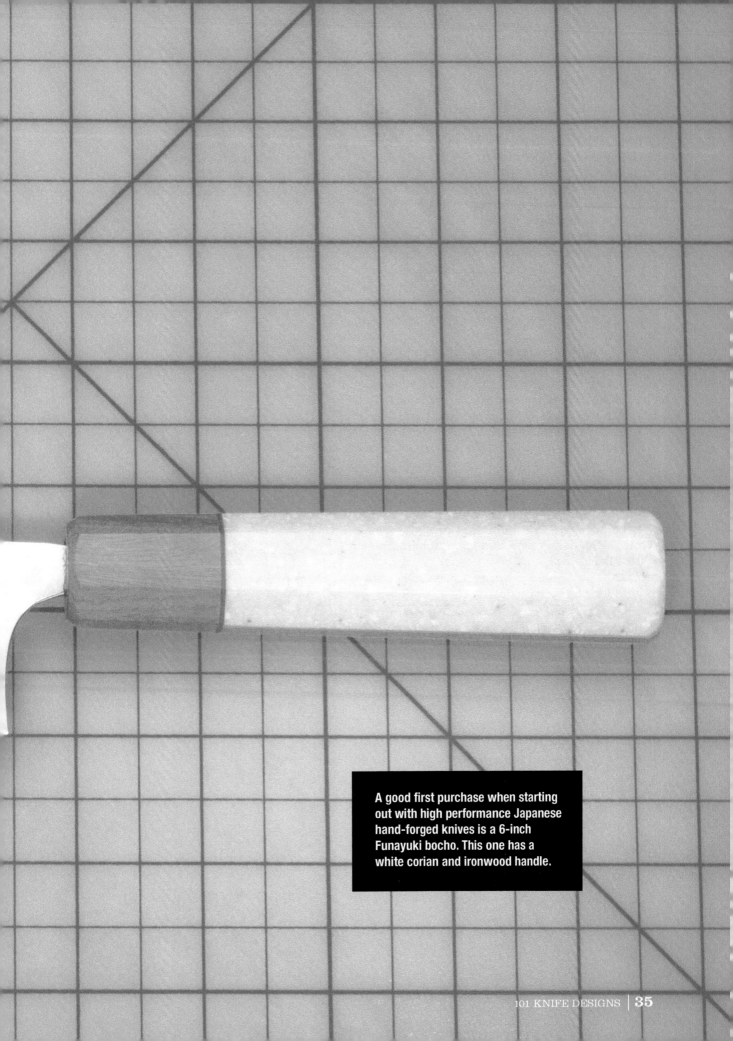

A good first purchase when starting out with high performance Japanese hand-forged knives is a 6-inch Funayuki bocho. This one has a white corian and ironwood handle.

Slicing Knives

Slicing knives are the most common of all kitchen knives. This category includes French style chef knives, Japanese chef knives, Chinese knives (see side bar essay on the Tsai Dao), boning knives, carving knives, long thin slicing knives and bread knives. The common trait is that they all are predominantly used in a fore/aft slicing motion. For some food prep such as mincing herbs, several of the slicing knives can be used in a controlled and precise manner to actually chop food on a cutting board.

Serrated slicing knives are fairly common in the Western kitchen. Serrations prevent blades from cutting as well as they theoretically could and also inhibit regular sharpening by the owner. In my opinion, the only knife in this category that benefits from serrations is the bread knife. Fresh bread straight out of the oven, especially French bread with hard crust, is best cut with a serrated bread knife. However, the crust of most other breads softens after a few hours out of the oven and it better sliced with a razor sharp straight edge.

An important design consideration for good kitchen slicing knives is not to let the blades get tip-heavy with extended length. They should feel balanced in the hand for prolonged use. This is the reason most wide kitchen knives with blades over six inches taper towards the tip, although some slicing knives have sharp points for piercing by design.

Please re-read the list of common traits of well-designed kitchen knives above and note the first trait: good kitchen knives are easy to sharpen! As a bladesmith or knifemaker, make kitchen knives thinner than you feel you should, especially thinning them out behind the primary cutting edge.

Chinese Tsai Dao

The traditional Chinese food prep knife is called the "Chinese cleaver" in English and "Tsai Dao" in Mandarin. Rather than have different shaped knives for various cutting tasks, the Chinese use similarly shaped blades of varying thickness and weight for different tasks. Some are very heavy cleavers for chopping through bones, while others have thin blades for slicing softer food. Many non-Chinese chefs who have made the effort to master these blades enjoy the versatility that they offer.

The classic Japanese Kitchen knife pattern: a Wabocho (also known as a Santoku). A custom fit octagonal cocobolo and olive wood handle complements this svelte knife. In the background is the registry for Mitsu Boshi Higo Masamune (Three Stars, Kumamoto Masamune) dating back generations of Yoshimoto bladesmiths.

Commemorative blades for Rawhyde
Adventures BMW GS Motorcycle Rid-
ing school in California where Carter
Cutlery filmed "High Performance
Tips".

RawHyde
Adven

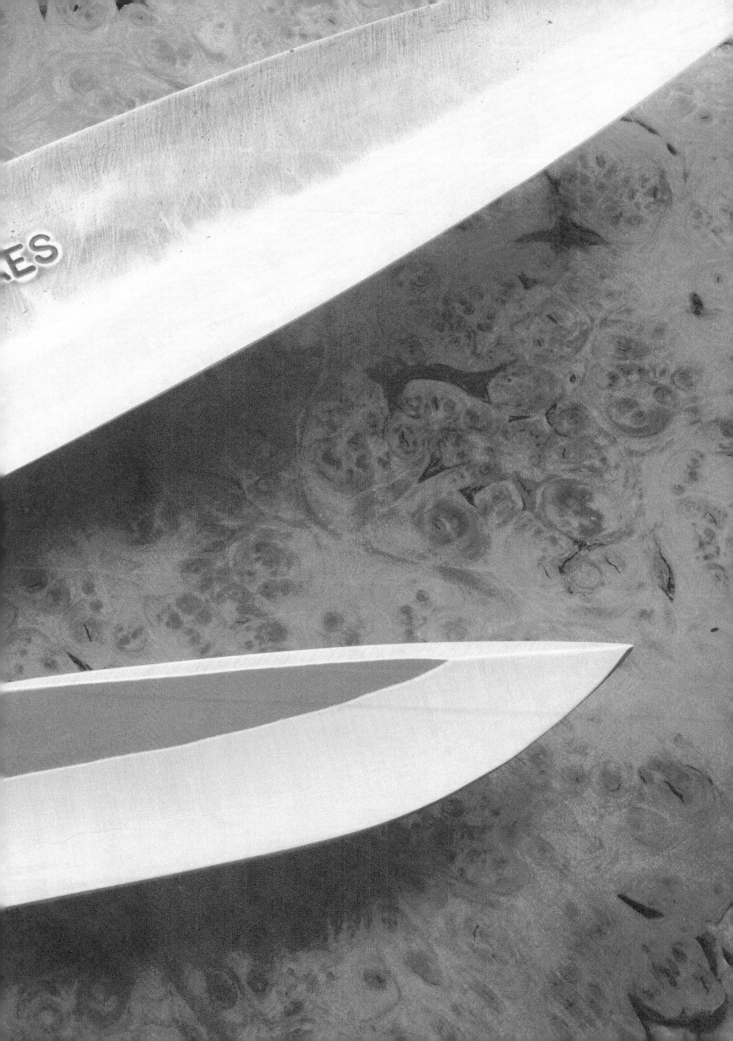

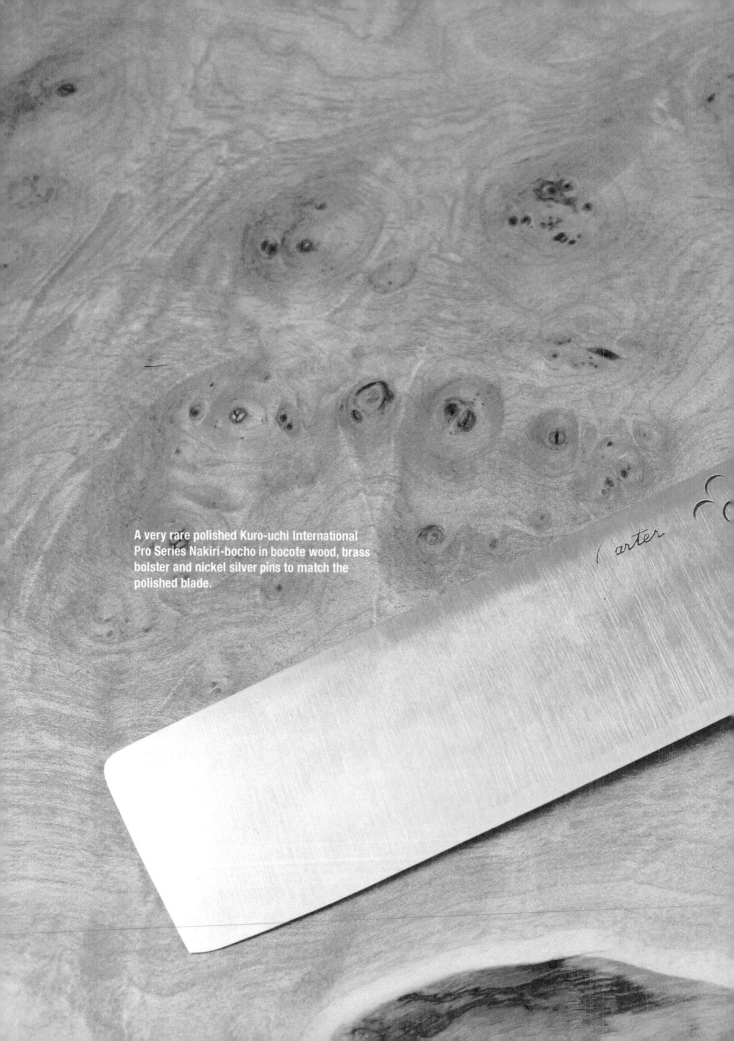

A very rare polished Kuro-uchi International Pro Series Nakiri-bocho in bocote wood, brass bolster and nickel silver pins to match the polished blade.

Chopping Knives, a.k.a Cleavers

Remember that a chopping motion is forcing a blade straight into the medium with no fore/aft blade motion. Due to the forces involved, chopping blades must be stout enough to resist edge failure during use. That said, consider the Japanese Nakiri-bocho, a rectangular blade used for chopping veggies, superior examples of which are no thicker than 1.2 mm at the thickest part of the blade. The primary edges of many of these knives are easily thin enough to shave the face with! If a thin-bladed knife is used for chopping, it must be perfectly heat-treated and the user must avoid undue pressure on the sides of the primary edge, such as those resulting from twisting or misaligned force to the blade.

Most chopping knives, except the aforementioned Japanese Nakiri-bocho, have more heft to them than slicing knives. In many cases the extra weight comes in the form of more mass out towards the tip of the blade. This extra weight out front gives the blade more momentum in motion to power through the material being cut. The Western cleaver is the most notable example that comes to mind. However, there is a direct correlation between the amount of weight forward and the inability of a blade to perform slicing tasks as well.

The Japanese Deba-bocho is a clever compromise as a hefty chopper that still has reasonable slicing ability.

Ultra-thin Nakiri-bocho can slice and chop if used with care.

Japanese Deba does it all –
slice, chop and pierce – but
at the cost of added weight.

Knives for Work, Hobbies and Outdoors

Utility Knives, Blades Four Inches and Less

Aside from culinary knives, the next most commonly used blades are small utility knives used by workers and hobbyists. Rarely will these knives have blades longer than four inches, and most will have smooth, simple profile handles. Small utility blades include a large spectrum of knives from scalpels to hunting knives and from pen knives to large folders. With few exceptions, this genre of knife is used primarily for slicing and used occasionally for piercing.

Thin, gentle curving edges with a well sharpened tip for precision work makes for an effective utility knife. Stout, heavy blades are not necessary due to the fact that these blades will rarely be pressed into chopping service. Of all the non-culinary knives, utility blades will definitely see the most use, and therefore it is of paramount importance that they be designed with ease of sharpening in mind. The dull utili-

For all around utility, it is hard to beat this **Wharncliffe Brute** model neck knife. Notice that the point lines up with the center of the blade to allow for piercing when necessary.

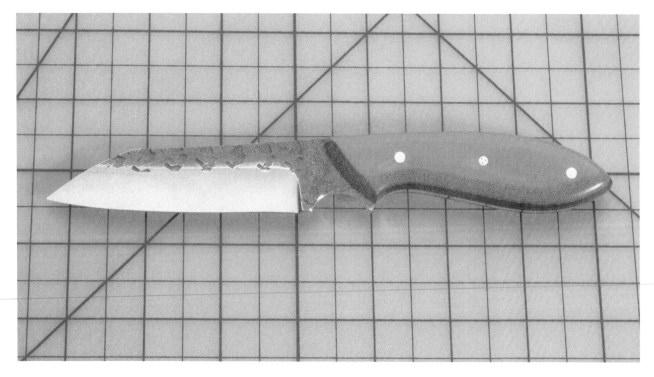

Blades with serrations or saw teeth make it practically impossible for average users to do regular sharpening and maintenance.

ty knife that is difficult to re-sharpen will be left behind when cutting chores abound. If it is not getting used to answer cutting tasks, one can hardly deem it a practical design. I'll add here that serrations on utility knives almost always render the knife useless once the serrations dull. Most users can't or won't re-sharpen them. Again, the knife starts to accumulate dust once the initial edge is gone.

As for the degree of point on the blade, and where the point falls in relation to the center of the blade, it is helpful to consider that, with few exceptions, the tips of these knifes are rarely used to stab deeply into a medium. Rather, the points are used for superficial tasks such as cutting out magazine articles, removing splinters or lancing a boil. The requirements of and forces affecting the point are physically different in small utility knives compared to larger combat and camp knives.

As the group of knives that gets more use than any other knives save culinary blades, it is extremely important for these knives to incorporate smooth, comfortable handles that are kind to the hands after hours of constant use. Generally speaking, the less distinct features in the handle, such as deep finger grooves or other sharp contours, the better. Slight off-set in the handle, curving slightly down and away in the direction of the cutting edge will result in less wrist fatigue over prolonged use. This will also help to instinctively index the blade in the hand for unsighted use. As I mentioned in my discussion about kitchen paring knives, when the handle on a utility knife allows the knife to be held in a variety of comfortable positions, it will be used constantly for a wide variety of cutting tasks. This constant and varied use will quickly lead to perfect familiarity, which leads to mastery of the tool. These smaller utility knives truly can become natural extensions of the user's hand.

Next to consider are metal finger guards on utility knives. A guard on a small utility knife is often a cosmetic feature to make the knife look larger and more capable than it really is. It mimics design of larger combat and camp knives. With the exception of some of the larger utility knives with upwards of 4-inch blades, guards are a hindrance to the user. While some claim a guard is a necessary safety measure, I disagree, pointing to guard-free traditional knives from around the world such as the Scandinavian Pukko and Japanese Kaiken. Awareness on the part of the user as to where the blade begins and ends, and subtleties in the handle for automatic safe indexing are all that is necessary to prevent mishaps.

If a utility knife is selected for field dressing game or farm animals, blades with clip points should be avoided and drop-point blades favored. The clip point blade is more likely to puncture the stomach and intestines of game during evisceration.

This simple "paring style" neck knife is plenty pointy for superficial piercing tasks and has a simple handle design that allows great grip flexibility. The knife features a stabilized olive wood handle and author's signature hammer-forged surface finish.

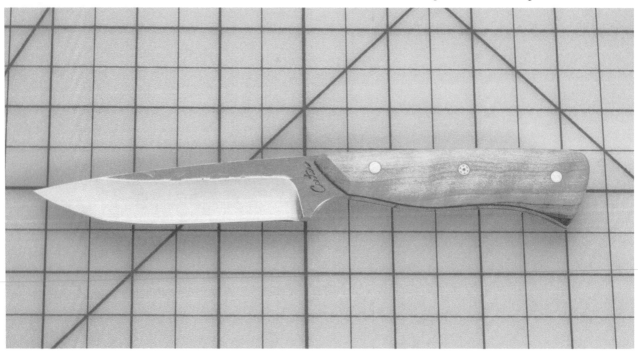

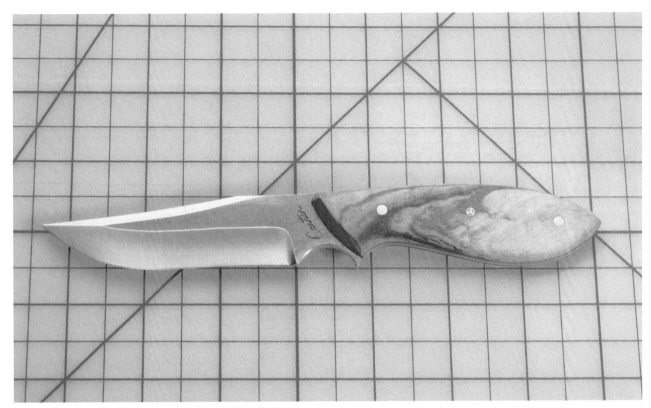

(above) Clave model neck knife with laminated blade and stabilized olive wood handle. Very stylistic knife with sharp point,
but not the best choice for field dressing game because extra
care must be taken not to inadvertently puncture the offal with
the clip point.

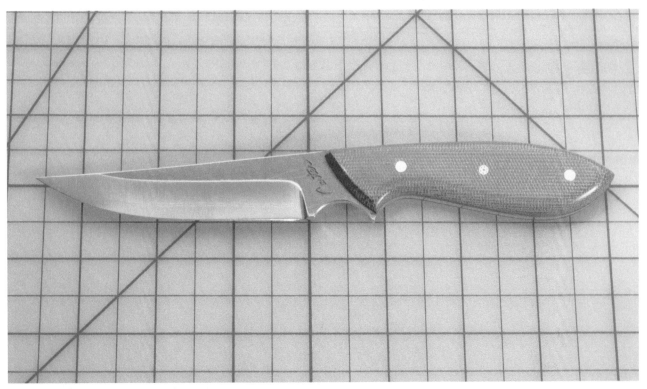

Persian model neck knife with laminated blade and tan canvas
micarta handle. This blade shape excels at slicing, but not at
field dressing game.

American Hunting Knife

Author and knife expert Bernard Levine outlines the history and development of the American hunting knife in his book Levine's Guide to Knives and Their Values, 2nd Edition. Levine states that the American hunting knife is "a recent creation that first appeared a little over a century ago." In the expert's opinion, "unlike pocket knives, butcher knives, or original Bowie knives, the modern American hunting knife is not intended for ordinary daily carry or use. It is a sportsman's knife intended for leisure-time pursuits." As to what exactly constitutes such a knife, it is, Levine continues, "a cross between the

This 5½-inch laminated blade with Sambar stag and brass handle will conceal better on the person than a full size 7-inch blade combat knife. The owner must know its limitations though for effective use.

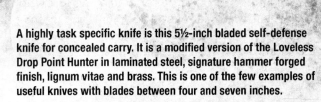

A highly task specific knife is this 5½-inch bladed self-defense knife for concealed carry. It is a modified version of the Loveless Drop Point Hunter in laminated steel, signature hammer forged finish, lignum vitae and brass. This is one of the few examples of useful knives with blades between four and seven inches.

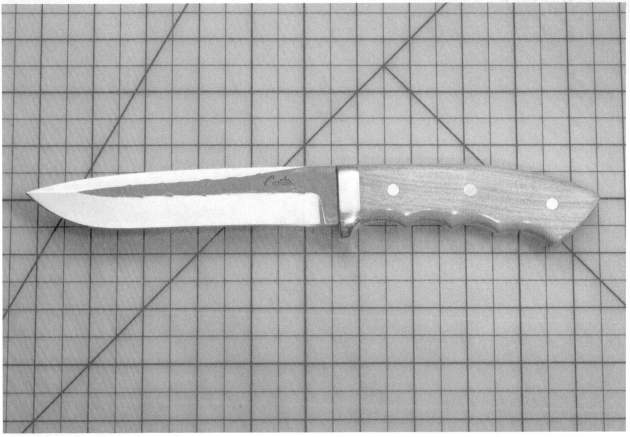

Bowie knife, which was primarily a weapon, and the butcher knife, which was used for skinning and cutting up game by frontiersmen, farmers and Indians."

Specifically referring to Bowie-Style hunting knives, Mr. Levine emphasizes that these knives are not used among serious sportsman and that they are not practical tools. "As butcher knives they are too big and thick. As brush knives they are not big enough. I suspect that they appealed to the city boy's dime novel fantasies about fighting a ferocious grizzly bear and rescuing a rancher's daughter."

Most American hunting knives fall into the "no-man's-land" blade size of between four and seven inches in length, a great and practical length for kitchen blades but almost useless elsewhere. One of the few applications for a blade this long is for self-defense when the owner desires the largest blade that can still be concealed on the person. As a bona fide weapon, a longer blade over seven inches is to be desired, but nearly impossible for most folks to conceal on their person. In a true "wilderness survival" situation, a light knife with a strong blade of at least seven inches should be selected.

Combat Knives, 7- to 9-Inch Blades

As the title implies, humans have been using knives both defensively and offensively against their fellow man since the beginning of time. Despite modern romantic notions by people who are far removed from actual combat, the primary function of this genre of knives is piercing, not slicing. The Roman soldiers learned millen-nia ago, and popularized the saying, "slice to wound, pierce to kill." As such, to dispatch an opponent, the blade must be sufficiently long enough to reach major internal organs, such as the heart, kidneys or liver, when thrust from any conceivable direction. The minimum length measures out to be seven inches. Longer blades offer better reach, but over 9-inch blades become less wieldy and cumbersome to carry into com-

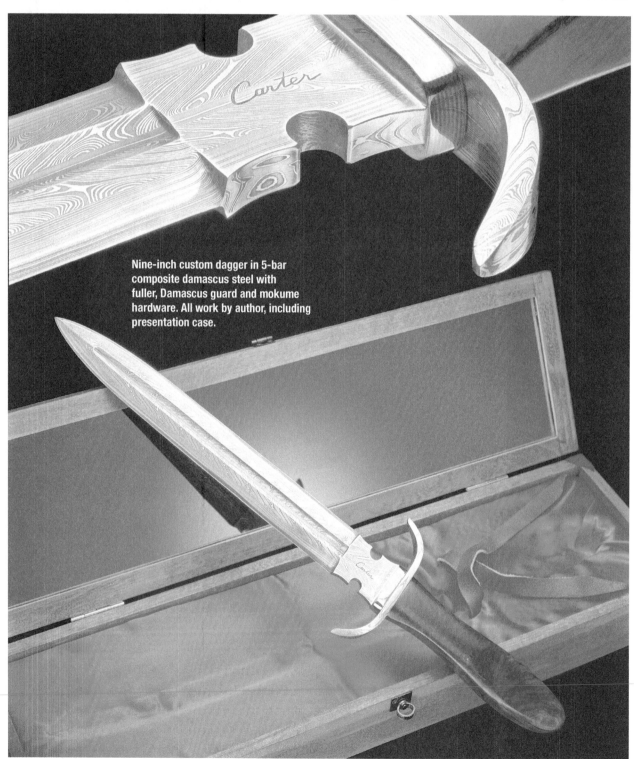

Nine-inch custom dagger in 5-bar composite damascus steel with fuller, Damascus guard and mokume hardware. All work by author, including presentation case.

(top left) The reality of carrying a long combat knife in the field is eye-opening. Here the sheath is seen 'flapping in the wind' when the owner runs. There just aren't that many places to wear it securely. Yes, the end of the sheath can be secured to the thigh with cord, but that presents some limitations as well.

(top rirght This knife is not only at risk for snagging in some brush, it is also noisy, slapping against the body with every right step. Tie it down, secure it elsewhere or get a smaller knife!

(right) Combat knife in use. An exposed neck would present a rare opportunity to use a combat knife for slicing. The more common application involves piercing deeply with the point multiple times.

Any blade with a point needs to be "thumbtack sharp." This premium Oyako model neck knife features a stabilized olive wood handle with red liners, two mosaic pins and six nickel silver pins.

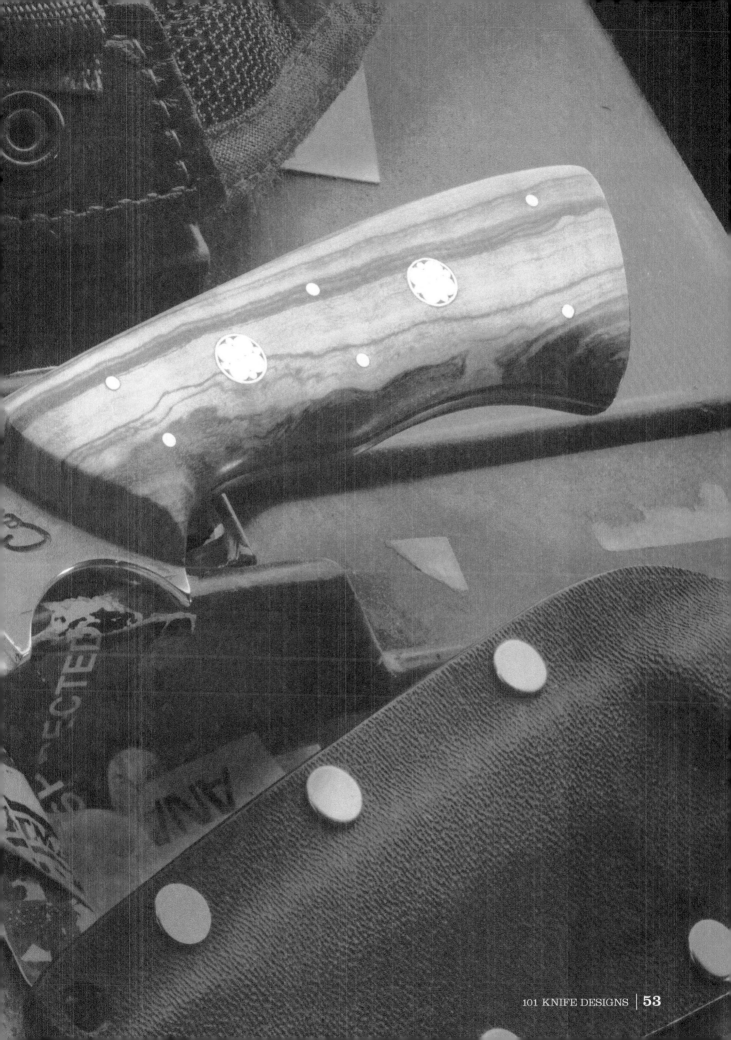

bat, considering average male heights between 5'9" and 6'3". (Obviously, comfortable knife sizes will vary with the owners' size.)

Knives designed purely for combat are primarily piercing blades and therefore the straightness of the entire blade, the position of the point, the sharpness of the point, the drag co-efficient and the strength-to-weight ratio are of paramount importance. As for the straightness of the blade, expert Burton says, "Remains now to consider... a weapon for point, a use to which, as its various shapes show, it was applied in the earliest ages instinctively, as it were, before Science taught the superiority of the thrust to the cut. We learn from such hand-thrusting instruments – the awl, gimlet, needle and dinner fork – that the straight weapon may be considered a very acute wedge with a method of progression mostly oblique. It is easy to prove that the proper shape for a thrusting-blade is pre-eminently the straight."

While many curved blades have been and are used for piercing, when compared to the physical effort required to pierce with a straight blade Burton continues, "with a proportionate loss of depth at the same expenditure of force.

(left) This is how the author tests the point on a blade; with light pressure the knife point should easily pick up the finger prints on the thumb and pull the skin lightly away. The pressure applied is so light there is absolutely no danger of hurting yourself. Anything less than a truly sharp point will just slide over the skin.

(right) Another view of the "thumbtack sharp" test. Try it with a pointy thumbtack first to get a feel for this test.

This augmented resistance to penetration is one, but only one, of the many difficulties in using a curved blade for a straight thrust."

Ideally, a task-specific piercing blade is shaped similar to a dagger. The dagger design places the point of the blade perfectly in the center of the blade. Not only does this allow for ideal piercing, but it enables both sides of the blade to have the same edge geometry. This allows for two cutting edges instead of one. Although slicing cuts are less effective in neutralizing a foe, when they are executed, the ability to slice in two directions has its advantages.

The sharpness of the point – the leading part of the blade that initiates piercing – is commonly overlooked. A properly sharpened point will be "thumbtack sharp," that is, the point will catch the fingerprint grooves in the thumb print when the point is brought into light contact with the thumb at about a 30 degree angle. A point thus sharpened will require exponentially less force to pierce than a point that looks pointy to the untrained eye, but is actually round. An easy test is to drag the tip lightly across a sheet of copy paper to see if it slices the paper with point pressure alone.

As with aerodynamics, each irregular surface or protrusion on an airplane or car will exponentially increase the drag. Likewise, on a piercing blade, the profile of the blade and grind lines should all be conducive to minimal drag. Daggers with "leaf"-shaped blades, i.e., recurved edges behind the forward third of the blade, produce less drag than straight blades of the same

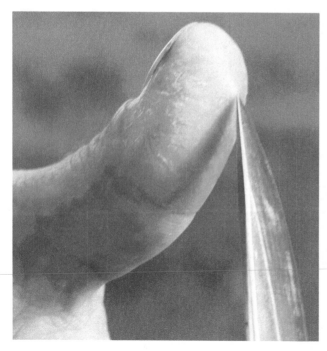
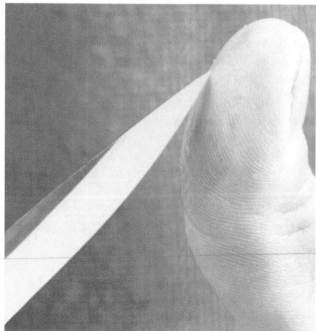

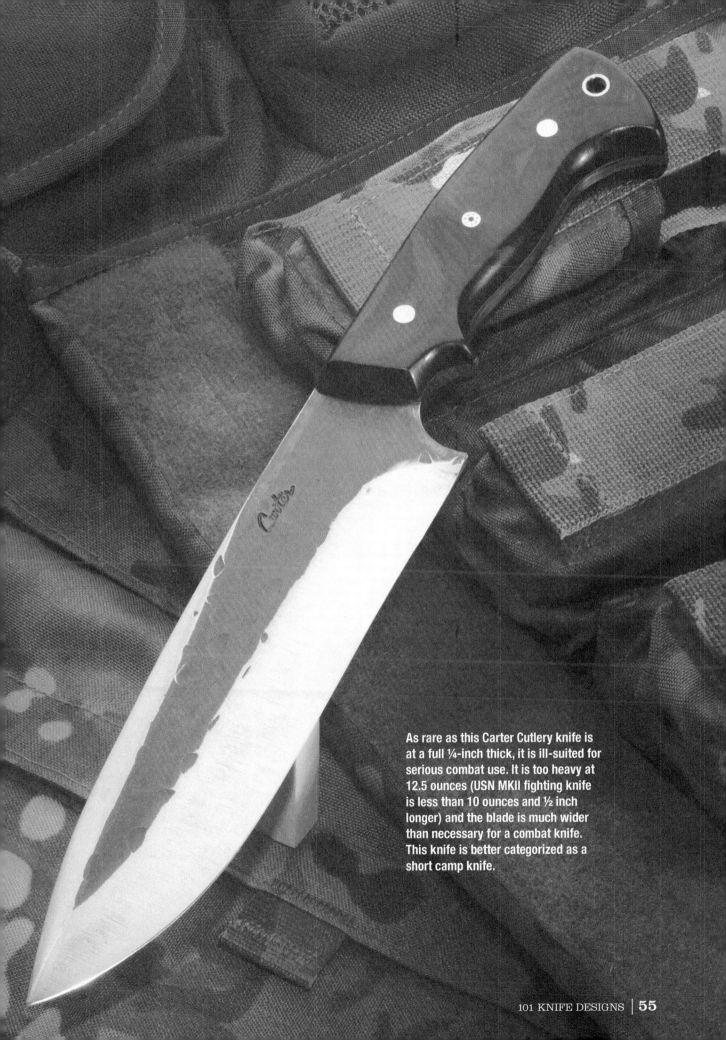

As rare as this Carter Cutlery knife is at a full ¼-inch thick, it is ill-suited for serious combat use. It is too heavy at 12.5 ounces (USN MKII fighting knife is less than 10 ounces and ½ inch longer) and the blade is much wider than necessary for a combat knife. This knife is better categorized as a short camp knife.

Master Your Combat Knife

The knife we use daily becomes a natural extension of our hand. Is it any wonder that most knife related crimes are committed with kitchen knives?

As I mentioned in my entries for kitchen paring knives and utility knives, ultimate mastery of a knife to the extent that it becomes a natural extension of the hand only results from constant daily use. Consider one day in the life of Murray Carter's Perfect model neck knife...

Wake up, put on my neck knife, get out of bed...spread peanut butter on my croissant and jam on my toast...cut out a coupon from the newspaper...pick stuck bacon from my teeth...open the mail....slice open the UPS boxes...pick a splinter from my finger...

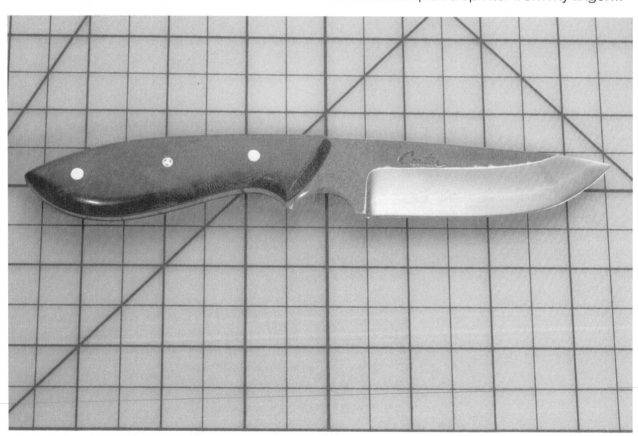

A right handed kata-ha (two layer laminate) version of the Original neck knife model...a Carter Cutlery classic! This one sports ironwood and red liners.

trim plastic ears from my child's "made in China" toy...mix some epoxy...scrape off excess epoxy...scribe a blade pattern...chop a one-inch branch from a tree...cut a pair of chopsticks from a branch to eat lunch...cut off excess silver solder from a soldered joint...skin a squirrel...dissect some coyote scat...wash the blade in soapy water...brake the passenger side window of an overturned car at the scene of an accident...cut some paracord for a customer's new neck knife... cut my steak... use the handle to tap loose the pickle lid... trim a loose thread from my pajamas and fondle the handle while I sit at my desk and write 101 Knife Designs!

Honestly, there have been many days like this in my neck knife's life and this is the way to master your knife. From this kind of varied use your hand will intuitively know how loose or firm to grasp the handle with different cutting tasks. There are no surprises like having the blade wrenched from your hand when impacting a hard material with speed.

If you truly want to master a larger "battle" blade, you will need to constantly carry it with you and find as many cutting tasks as you can to use it. Remember, a blade's practicality is commensurate with the amount of use it gets. This is why the Nepalese Khukri (Khukuri) is practical for a Ghurka warrior, but not for anybody else!

**(left) Just one of the many things I do daily with my neck knife.
(right) Just one gentle push is all it takes when you keep your knife razor sharp. Ease of sharpening is a criterion for practical blade design.**

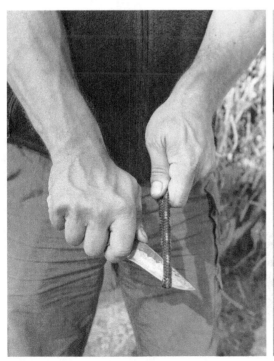
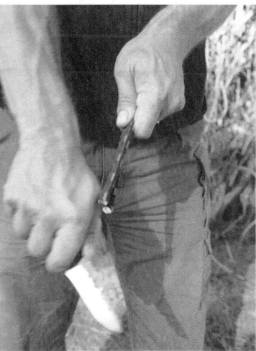

dimensions. Sharp plunge-cuts where a second edge begins half-way on the blade will produce areas of high drag, and possibly even snag the blade upon entry (see page 144). It goes without saying that saw-teeth on a combat blade indicate a total lack of understanding on the part of the designer.

Finally, not to be overlooked is the overall weight. The ideal combat knife will be extremely strong for its size with all excess weight trimmed off noncritical areas. At over 12 inches long including the handle, a blade this large is already a burden to carry for the soldier or adventurer who has to justify every ounce carried. Any knife considered "more knife than necessary" will simply get left behind and not be carried anywhere near conflict.

The bewildering question then begs to be asked: Why do so many so-called "combat knives" have wide single edges with false edges on the spine? The answer lies in the fact that what modern customers actually demand is a larger utility knife that could be pressed into combat if absolutely necessary. The single wide edge design is preferred because of its ability to slice and chop, which are tasks that are more commonly required of a soldier or adventurer during times other than lethal knife combat.

This avant garde "combat knife" design is benefited when successful design aspects of the dagger are applied, namely:

• A straight blade.

• A point that is near the center of the blade.

• A "thumbtack sharp" point.

Eleven-inch ladder pattern damascus camp knife with white steel core, damascus guard and sambar stag handle with damascus pommel. Plunge cuts are too sharp and will add drag when used in piercing (refer to page 144).

• A blade with little piercing drag and/or with a slightly recurved edge profile behind the first third of the blade.

• A size-to-weight ratio that makes it attractive to carry when ounces matter.

Camp Knives, 10- to 12-Inch Blades

Today's camp knives are modern versions of yesteryear's Bowie knives in terms of size and design as well as in spirit. The appeal of these knives harkens back to the days of American adventure in the early 1800s and stories of bravery during the American Civil War. Validating this claim is the fact that camp knives are primarily made and sold within the United States. A well-made and well-balanced camp knife is

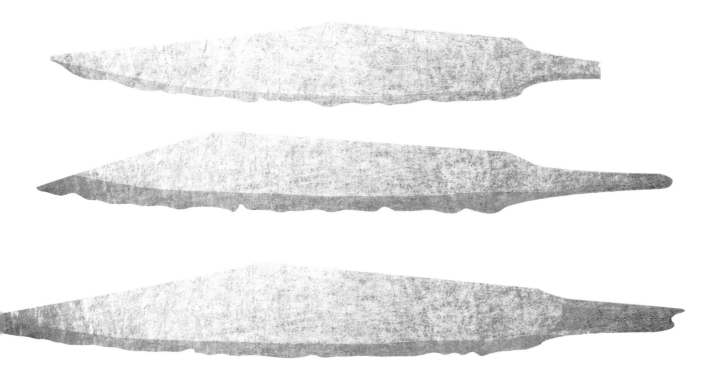

Predecessor to the Bowie Knife. Anglo-Saxon 'scramasax' blades dated to the 11th century, found in the Thames River, London, England. The blades are between eight and ten inches. (Page 36 Arms and Armor of the Medieval Knight). Note how the points line up perfectly with the center of the blades for piercing.

Japanese Matagi camp knife. Blade is 9¼ inch of Hitachi white steel #1/410 stainless laminate with desert ironwood handle. Carter Cutlery offers a version of this knife for hunting wild boar that has a point which lines up more closely with the center of the blade.

Batoning wood for the fire with the Japanese Matagi.

something to behold, and holding such a blade in one's hand stirs strong emotions. Even those with less than a casual interest in knives will feel the desire to chop something with a camp knife!

This genre of knife has enjoyed resurgence over the past 40 years after it was popularized by American Bladesmith Society founding member Bill Moran. The camp knife is by design a chopper. Its forte is chopping limbs of wood or of flesh with equal aplomb. As such, these knives typically are too heavy to be carried in the field by anyone, save hard-core aficionados, and many hand-made versions are too dear to risk banging around in the bush.

The piercing ability of camp knives varies by design, but those with sharp points located somewhere near the center of the blade would be adequate, provided the wielder of such a heavy knife could accurately guide the point to the intended target. Practical application of the camp knife for most users is when car-camping and equipment weight is not a factor. At such a campsite the camp knife can be used primarily for procuring small firewood and tinder. Another application might be for home protection by devoted knife enthusiasts who live in jurisdictions where firearms are restricted. Interestingly, blades closely resembling camp knives have been dated back to at least the 11th century.

Making tinder is an easy job with the Matagi knife.

Machetes, 16- to 20-Inch Blades

Machetes, which are also known as cutlasses in some parts of the world, are typically very thin-bladed tools for chopping vegetation, but are also used as hacking weapons in regions where firearms are not available. Machetes are subject to high impact stress during regular use so tough, spring-like blade qualities are desirable. A search around the world will reveal hundreds of common patterns with this genre of knife, so design isn't very restrictive. Machete blades are usually wide enough to provide adequate strength for the thin blades and also to withstand years of repetitive sharpening. When more momentum is desired, more weight will be present towards the tip of the blade.

Cutting down corn stalks is a piece of cake with author's Japanese laminated steel machete.

Carter Cutlery Kopis machete in Hitachi white steel #1 laminate and black canvas micarta with red liners. Overall length: 22½ inches.

Swords, Blades Over 20 Inches

Swords are cool. They are extremely difficult for the bladesmith to create and bladesmiths from ages past are to be revered. If holding a well-made camp knife evokes deep emotions, then the sword does so tenfold. Richard F. Burton's work The Book of the Sword is a fascinating and extremely educational read, and I have quoted him extensively in this work as his research findings applied to shorter blades. However, with that being said, I cannot, with a clear conscience, include swords in a book about practical design. Perhaps a book in the future about my own unique research on Japanese swords will be in order. In the meantime, let's stay focused on the topic at hand...practical knife designs!

Katana made by author's teacher's father, the 15th Generation Yoshimoto Bladesmith. This was presented to Murray when he was asked to become the 17th Generation smith and thus carry on over 400 years of uninterrupted bladesmithing.

In Typical Government Fashion

I don't fancy myself a knife collector, but one knife I have had since my youth, and the one I will always keep, is my grandfather's original issue USN MKII, made by Camillus, NY, in 1944, during WWII. As a child I was fascinated by this knife, the 7-inch blackened clip-point blade with fullers, the sculpted steel cross guard and the leather washer stacked handle with grooves and round steel pommel. The sheath was impressive as well…not the flimsy leather sheathes, but the genuine hard fiber and metal sheath. I was sure that a young man could go anywhere in the world with this knife and survive just fine, because the knife was just THAT good. (I held that opinion of this knife until Buck Knives released the BuckMaster in 1984!)

Clip points on these two highly prolific knives are of very poor design. The clip points prevent the blades from being truly efficient piercing knives.

In Typical Government Fashion [CONTINUED]

(above) **Author regrinds the point on a USN MKII Fighting knife on the Japanese rotating water stone sharpener.**

(below) **Author regrinds the profile on a USN MKII Fighting knife on the Japanese rotating water stone sharpener.**

However, that was then, and this is now. After making more than 17,000 knives and sharpening more than 70,000 knives during my career, I realize that the MKII fighting knife was obviously designed by someone with a poor understanding of practical blade design. I am referring specifically to the clip-point design, which offers no cutting advantages but does seriously impair effective use of the blade as a piercing weapon.

It appears the designers of this blade were mimicking a common design feature of Bowie style blades to appeal to romantic notion rather than practical considerations. I concur with my colleague and fellow ABS Mastersmith, Ed Fowler of Riverton, WY,

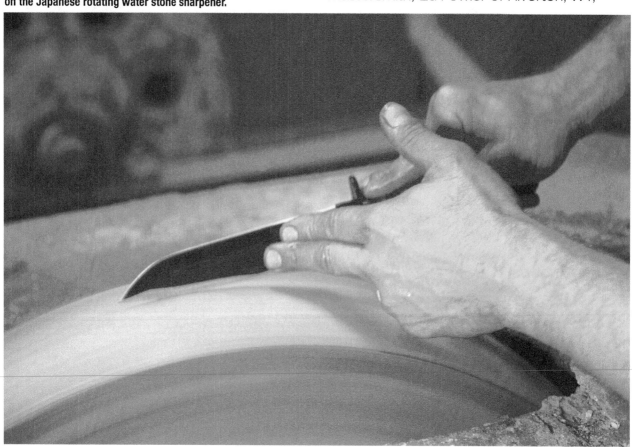

when he states in his book Knife Talk, "...I finally concluded that the men who designed knives for the military, the men who purchased knives for the military and the men who made knives for the military were not all primarily concerned with making the best tool for the job. Some of them may have thought they were providing the best knife for the job [but] they just didn't know any better. Others were more concerned with profit or their egos."

Another fatal design flaw in the vintage MKII fighting knives was the straight-line, perfectly round handle. This handle design prevents the user from being able to instinctively 'index' the knife in their hand without first visually confirming what direction the cutting edge of the blade is pointed. To illustrate this problem I have a skeptic close their eyes and place their hand in front of them

Author regrinds the false edge (chamfer) on a USN MKII Fighting knife on the Japanese rotating water stone sharpener.

ready to accept the knife, which I place in their hands. I place the knife in their hands so that the cutting edge is any direction but in front of them. I then instruct them, with their eyes still closed, to cut an imaginary cake in front of them. The blade can never be correctly lined up to make the cut because the handle gives no clues to the hand where the edge is pointed.

Handles which are slightly oval in cross-section and slightly curved down towards the end of the handle enable the user to instinctively position the blade with the cutting edge in line with the direction of movement. Newer MKII style fighting knives, also with stacked leather washer handles, are contoured more in an oval shape, thus somewhat improving this design flaw. Even so, this prolific American military icon exemplifies the worst result that government bureaucracy can produce.

USN MKII Fighting knife before and after regrinding of the tip. The regrind takes Murray just a few minutes but vastly improves the piercing performance of the blade.

(above) Communist AK-47 bayonet. I guess if you want to lose the Cold War, then it makes sense to design a bayonet with saw teeth to get caught up in the enemy during use.

(left) Author regrinds a Russian AK-47 bayonet on the Japanese rotating water stone sharpener.

A simple modification to a bad design goes a long way to improve its practicality.

Perhaps the most ironic and hilarious blunder of governmental failure is manifested in the Russian AK-47 bayonet design. Designed during the cold war when Russia was opposed to all things American, they copied the American clip-point design in the blade, which limited its effectiveness in piercing and demonstrated to the world their envy of Americana. The AK bayonet design may have been the surest sign that the U.S. was going to win the cold war.

(left) Author regrinds the chamfer (false edge) on the AK-47 bayonet using the Japanese rotating water stone sharpener.

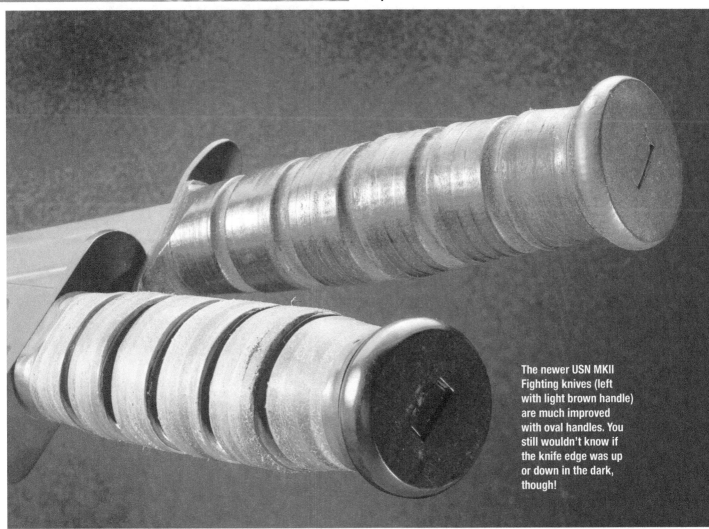

The newer USN MKII Fighting knives (left with light brown handle) are much improved with oval handles. You still wouldn't know if the knife edge was up or down in the dark, though!

Dreaming About Knives: Can You Relate?

From ABS Master Bladesmith Ed Fowler in Knife Talk: "Fact is, I eat, sleep, breathe and dream knives. It doesn't matter whether I am irrigating, branding or pulling a calf. Likely as not a knife is on my mind. When I see a beautiful lady, I want to make a knife that looks and works like her. That is my dream – knives!"

Can you relate?

When it comes to looking at knives and seeing what is there, few see to the depths that Ed does.

Author often finds himself thinking about the next batch of knives he is going to forge. This slick Tactical model neck knife was forged out of Hitachi White steel #1 and stainless laminate and wears ebony handles with white liners.

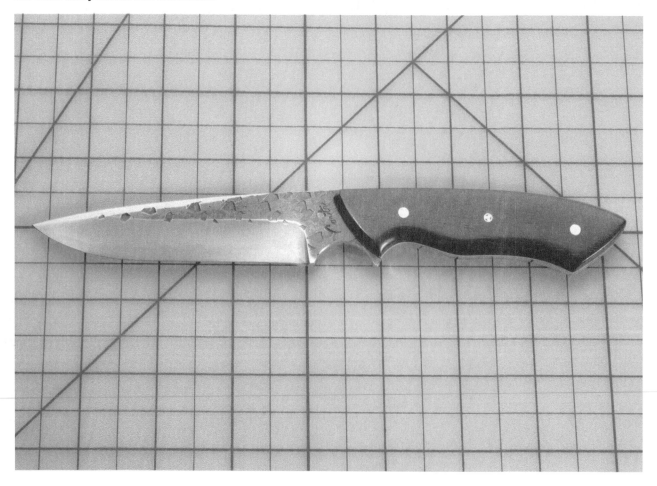

(left) Cutting out blades from the forged billets on a circular chop saw. Even after 17,000 knives, Murray is still excited to see how the next knife is going to turn out.

Far in the background, author dreams about making knives while he sits, mesmerized by the fire.

(below) Working with the power hammer is kind of like piloting a helicopter for a living, dangerous but downright exciting. Here the author cold forges a blade prior to quenching.

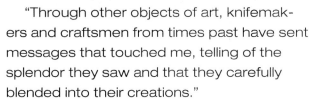

"Through other objects of art, knifemakers and craftsmen from times past have sent messages that touched me, telling of the splendor they saw and that they carefully blended into their creations."

And following is one more quotation that illustrates the similarities in blade philosophy between my good friend Ed Fowler and I:

"Sharpening is your opportunity to develop a skill and take over where the knifemaker leaves off. Sharpening is your signature on your knives."

Thanks, Ed, for your wonderful contributions to the cutlery industry!

Classic Knife Designs

In a phone interview with Joe Kertzman, author of *Art of the Knife* and several years of Knives annuals, and managing editor at BLADE Magazine, I asked what knife designs he thought were classics, and which patterns have stood the test of time. Joe listed the following:

- Boot Knife /dirk/daggers/Italian Stiletto.
- Buck model 110 folder.
- Laguoile folding knives of France.
- Bowie Knife/D-guard Bowie Knife.
- Kopis design, specifically the Nepalese Ghurka Kukri.
- Loveless Drop Point hunter.
- Cleaver/axe.
- Javanese Kris and other wavy blades.

Let's examine Joe's choices, in light of their classification according to size and also in light of what features the blades manifest in terms of slicing, chopping or piercing. Why would an expert, who is familiar with literally thousands of various types of knives, name these few off the top of his head when surprised with the question? I think the answer is clear. Let's expound...

Joe's first mention, the boot knife, dirk, dagger and stiletto must actually be divided up into two categories: the boot knife and dirk which average between three and five inches in blade length, and daggers and stilettos which fall into our combat knife category.

Boot knives and dirks fall into a size category that I call "no man's land" because they are usually longer than utility knives and lack much utilitarian use, but fall a couple inches short as being effective combat knives. The only practical application for such a knife is when it is desirable to carry the largest possible bladed weapon concealed on the person. While this size and style of knife sells fairly well on the market, the truth is that not many of the boot knives sold are ever pressed into daily service. Their popularity, despite the lack of practicality, derives from the fact that they mimic their large, more effective brothers, daggers and stilettos, which really are classics. These knives have existed since the discovery of metal and are solely designed for the purpose of piercing. These classic blades do what they were designed to do exceptionally well, which is why they are so popular the world over.

From left to right: Boot knife, dirk, dagger and stiletto.

(opposite) Carter Cutlery's "Ultimate" utility knife, the Wharncliffe Brute neck knife. This knife has incredible slicing power for its size, is easy to maintain and easy to sharpen. This blade design surpasses a conventional drop point blade design in all tasks with the one exception of skinning game. Otherwise, it is THE 'go to' blade.

I'll discuss the next two entries together: the Buck 110 and the Laguiole folding knives. Although these two knives are produced thousands of miles apart and separated by the Atlantic Ocean, they are close to being exactly the same cutting answer to similar cutting demands. Both fall into the Utility knife category and are made primarily for slicing. Both blades feature sharp points for superficial piercing work, are thin and easy to re-sharpen. Neither blade has the mass or weight required for chopping.

Of the two knives, the Laguiole has a better-designed blade due to the straight spine section down to the tip and also sporting a very slight recurve in the cutting edge one third of the way back from the tip. The Buck 110 has a Bowie style clip point which has aesthetic appeal but no practical function. The overall light weight and folding design makes these knives useful slicers to just about anyone. Millions of these knives and their variants are carried daily in every corner of the world to accomplish ordinary cutting chores.

The next entry on Joe's list is the American Bowie Knife and D-shaped Guard Bowie. Categorically, in terms of blade length these two fall somewhere between the Combat knife and Camp knife. However, if weight is to be a determining factor, then the two definitely belong in the camp knife class. Since at least the 11th century, this class of knife has been popular as a secondary weapon, and only since the development of reliable repeating handguns has the knife fallen out of common use. These chopping and sometimes thrusting knives remain popular today amongst makers and collectors for their aesthetic value. The Bowie and its variants might just well be the best compromise ever in a fighting blade that combines chopping, piercing and slicing. Furthermore, because of their use in early American history, this genre of knife has become an American cultural icon, as important as ice cream and apple pie.

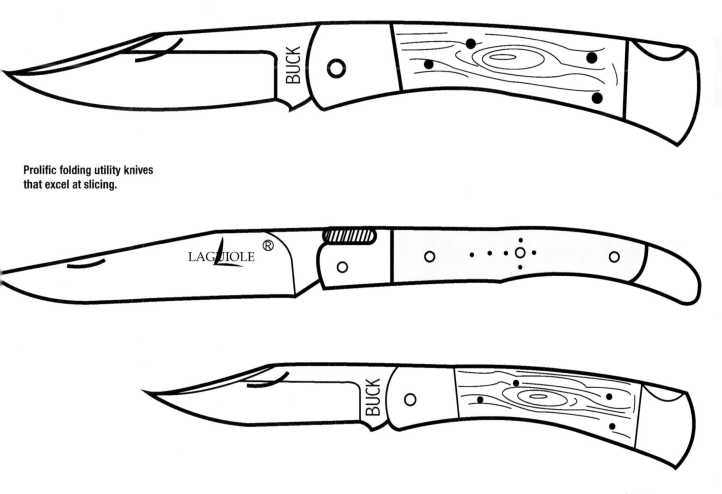

Prolific folding utility knives that excel at slicing.

(opposite) American icon: the Bowie Knife. A) Perhaps the pattern that comes to mind when the word Bowie Knife is mentioned. This pattern has a well-positioned point for piercing, and plenty of width and heft for chopping. Although accepted as historically correct, the interrupted line from spine to handle is not as smooth flowing as the other four knives pictured. B) The wide curved blade in this example gives us some insight into the intention of the bladesmith who forged this beauty. It is clearly made for chopping and slicing, but with a pointy tip for superficial piercing. The contoured handle is a very nice touch. C) This knife is patterned from a meat carving/slicing knife. The trailing point is not efficient at piercing, but sure does look menacing. The length alone would frighten many an enemy away, but at the same time would present carry challenges. D) Searles Bowie Knife. With Mediterranean influence, this hefty chopper also has an in-line point with the handle for effective piercing. The tiny gap between the heel of the blade and the guard presents a nightmare to keep free of rust and gunk. E) D-Guard Bowies became popular with Confederate troops during the American Civil War. This pattern has a nicely positioned point for piercing and a curved blade for slicing. The D-guard would have offered the ability to land some devastating punching blows, as well as added security for the hand when burying the blade up to the hilt in an opponent. Disadvantages include limiting the grip positions when using as well as the fact that the guard would catch up in every little branch and bush when running through the woods with the knife in the sheath. For these reasons this pattern is not in production today.

Next is the Kopis design, which dates back to the Greek empire, but perhaps the most widely known pattern being the Nepalese Ghurka soldier's Kukri knife. These single-handed knives with tip-heavy, recurved blades are first and foremost chopping blades. The curved portion of the blade allowed for some slicing action, but its outstanding chopping power relative to its size is legendary. It is claimed that the tips of these knives could be used to pierce, but the combination of thickness of the blade near the tip, the bad alignment of the handle to tip and the lack of a guard or device to keep the hand from sliding up the sharpened portion of the blade upon impact limit the piercing effectiveness of this weapon. Adding to the blade's reputation is the warrior that is associated with it – the fierce Gurkha warrior who would rather die than surrender. They were feared by their enemies and admired by their allies.

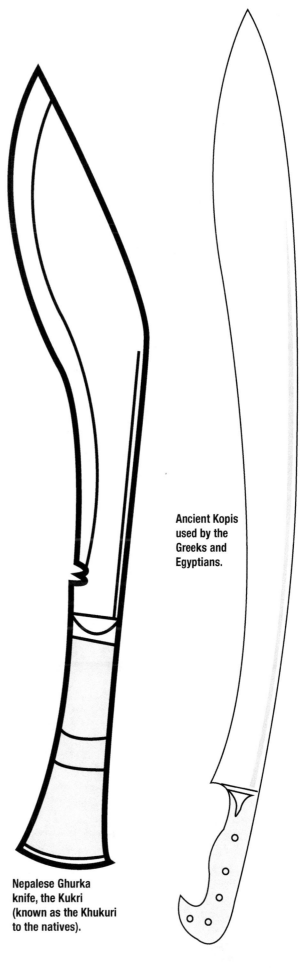

Ancient Kopis used by the Greeks and Egyptians.

Nepalese Ghurka knife, the Kukri (known as the Khukuri to the natives).

Author's version of the Loveless 4-inch Drop
Point Hunter in White steel #1/410 Stainless
laminate, black buffalo horn and brass hardware.
The finger grooves are shallow enough to allow
different grip configurations, but add to the
overall visual appeal. Practically speaking, a
smooth handle is better on this genre of knife.

▲ R.W.LOVELESS
maker
Riverside, Calif. ▲

Modern American icon;
the Loveless 4-inch
Drop Point Hunter.

Joe's mention of the Bob Loveless style of drop point hunter is fitting as it the single most copied knife by custom knifemakers in the past forty years. Features that make this design a classic are:

• Drop point blade under four inches

• Excellent curvature in the blade for superior slicing

• High secondary edge grind for keen cutting and ease of sharpening

• No jimping or choil to catch on what's being cut

• A minimal protruding guard that doesn't extend above the back of the spine

• A simple smooth handle with few protrusions

• Simple handle contour and slight bend that naturally indexes itself in the hand.

The Loveless design is a superb field dressing knife for large game and, as the most commonly copied knife in the world, has earned itself classic status in a relatively short time.

"When a man picks up a knife, there's an old memory from the collective unconscious that surfaces. A knife is an atavistic experience. It was man's first tool and weapon. Man was chipping flint into cutting edges before he invented the wheel. No matter how sophisticated we become, a knife takes us back to the cave." Bob Loveless

Cleaver and axes need little explanation. They epitomize blades expressly designed to chop. And chop they indeed do well.

Interestingly, I concur with Joe that the wavy blade pattern of the Javanese keris as well as the medieval two-handed long flame-bladed swords of Germany from the 1500s is a classic shape, although not a very practical design. The waves in the blade are designed to increase the slicing surface area, and as such were powerful slicers. Unfortunately, the difficulty of construction and sharpening challenges doomed this design to the exotic realm only. I think this exotic element is what captures people's imagination and that these blades were the predecessors of the fantasy knife movement.

In conclusion, I think it is obvious why my friend Joe Kertzman chose these classic knives; each genre of knife excels at slicing (folding knives, Loveless, keris), chopping (cleavers, axes), piercing (dirks, daggers) or in the case of the Bowie/camp knives, an effective combination thereof.

Javanese keris (also known as a kris).

The finest axes in the world come from Tosa, Koichi Prefecture, Japan. This is Murray's personal axe that he uses to chop wood to start the forge at work.

Long Original Neck Knife in stabilized olive wood.

Rope-handled Kiridashi belonging to my trusty admin assistant. This knife gets used daily.

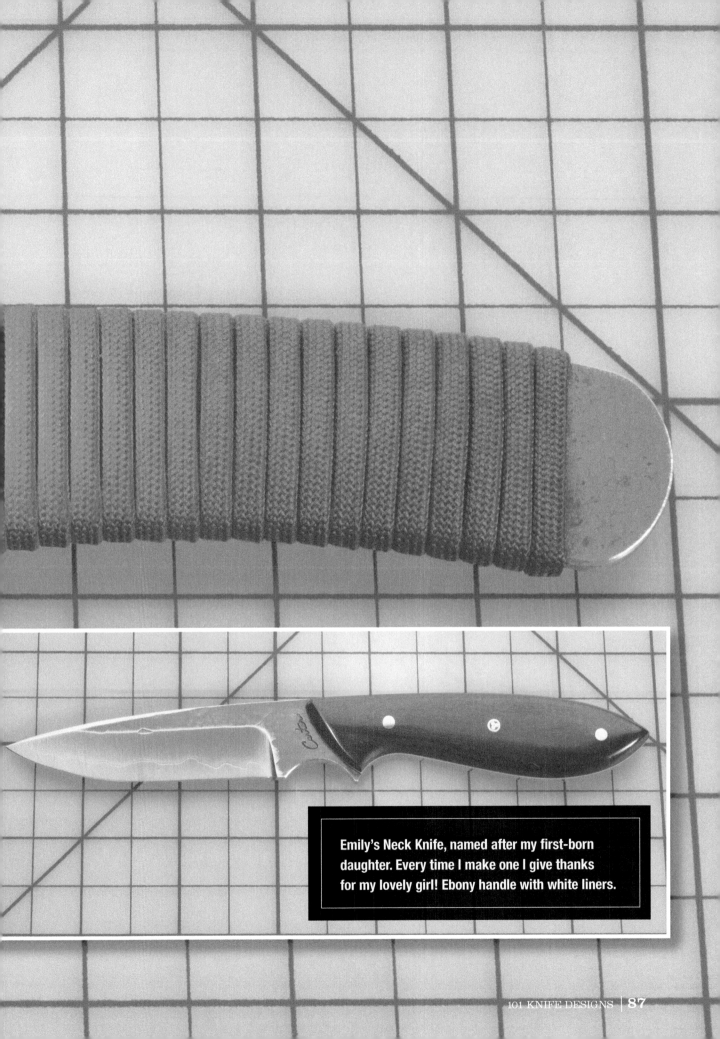

Emily's Neck Knife, named after my first-born daughter. Every time I make one I give thanks for my lovely girl! Ebony handle with white liners.

A prototype mini Wharncliffe Brute in lignum vitae.

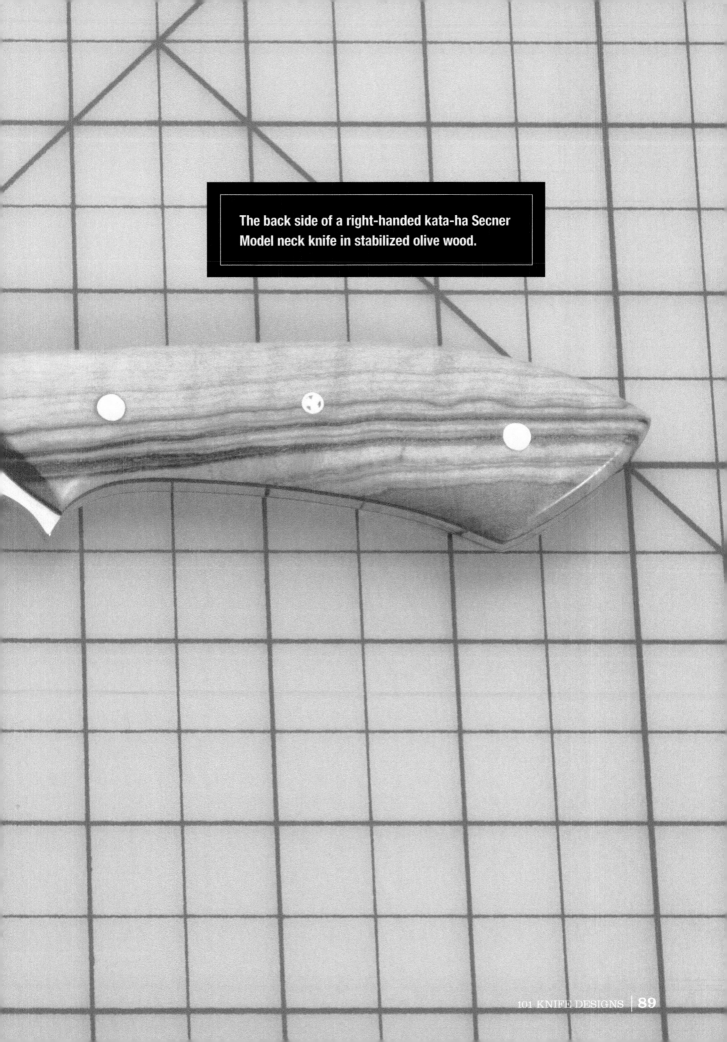

The back side of a right-handed kata-ha Secner Model neck knife in stabilized olive wood.

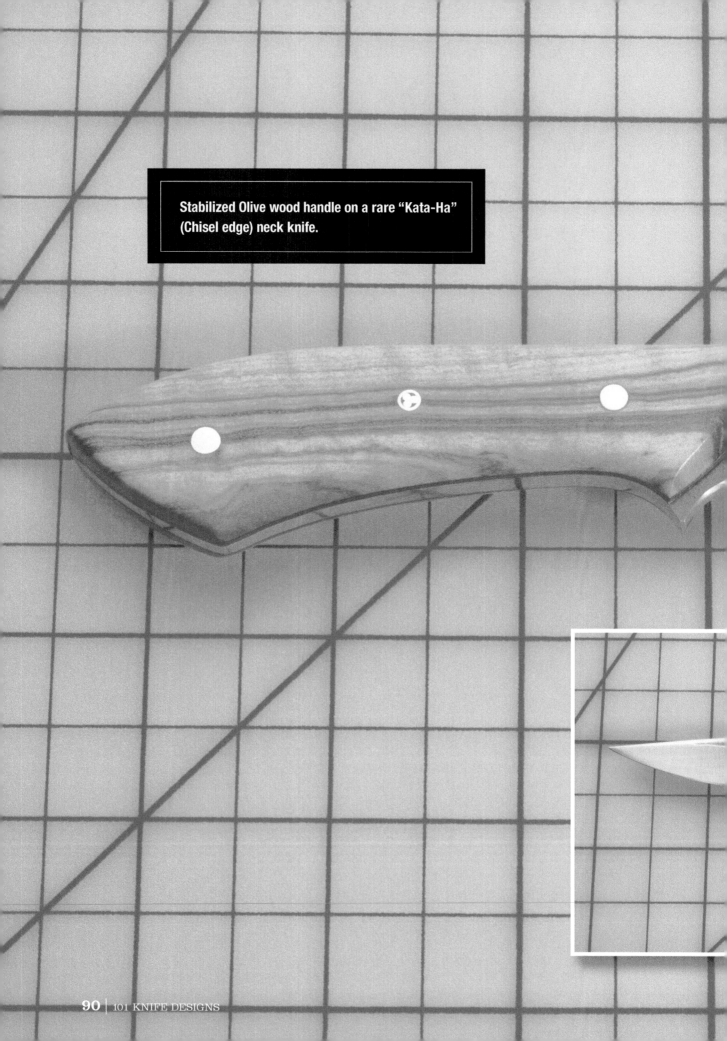

Stabilized Olive wood handle on a rare "Kata-Ha" (Chisel edge) neck knife.

Executive Neck knife wearing Macassar ebony scales.

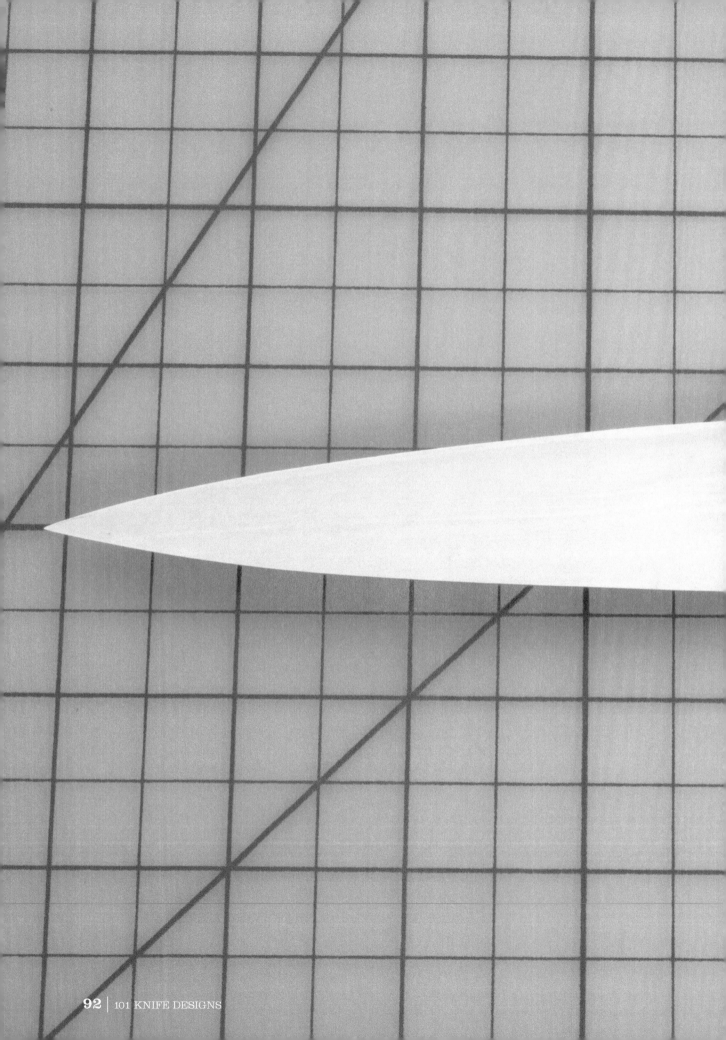

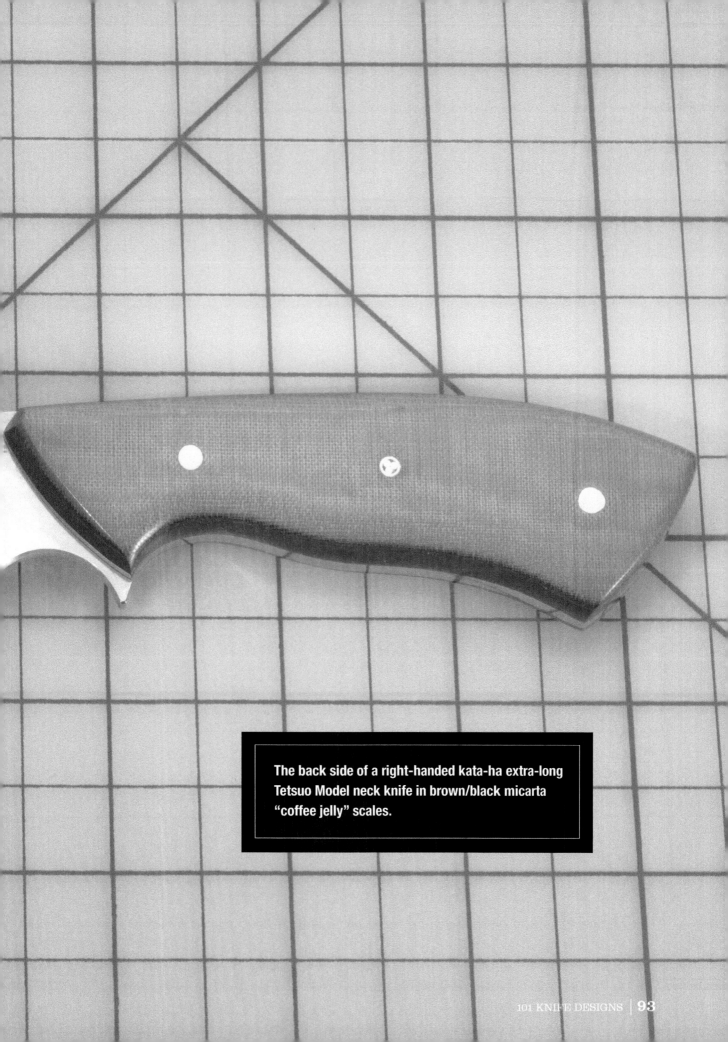

The back side of a right-handed kata-ha extra-long Tetsuo Model neck knife in brown/black micarta "coffee jelly" scales.

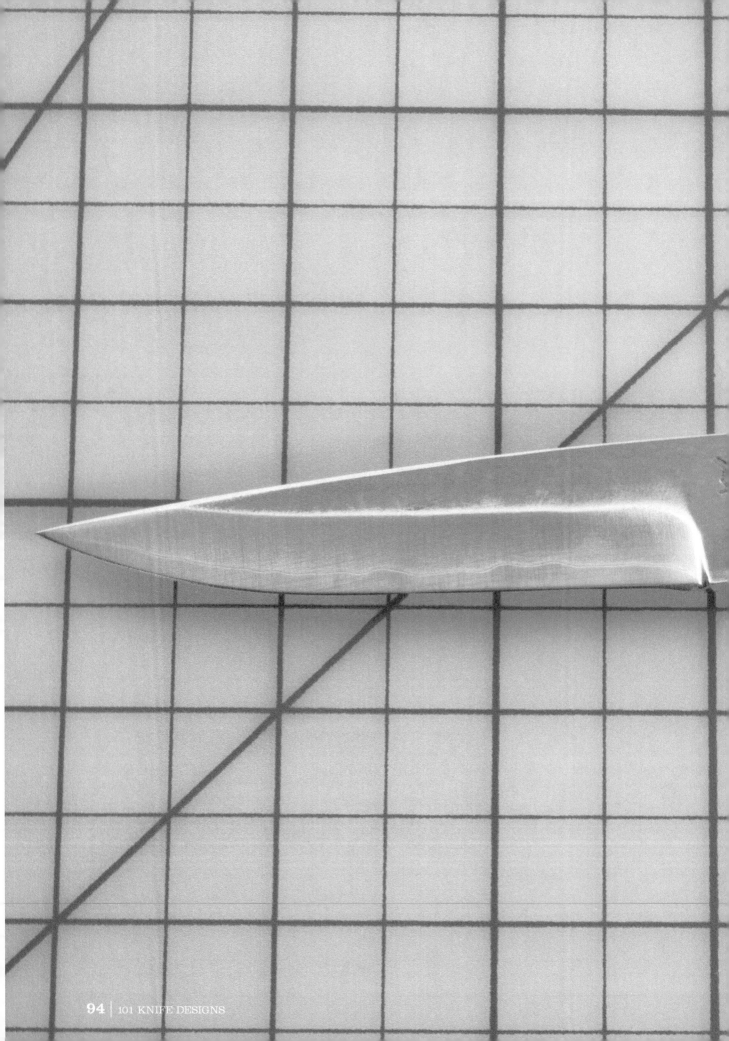

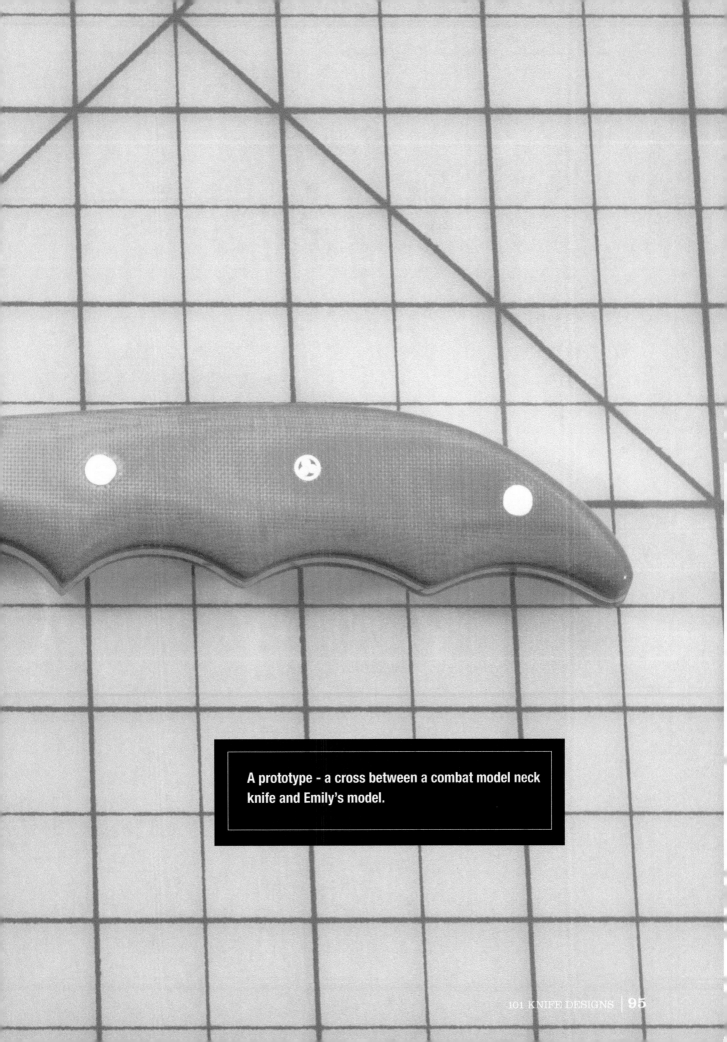

A prototype - a cross between a combat model neck knife and Emily's model.

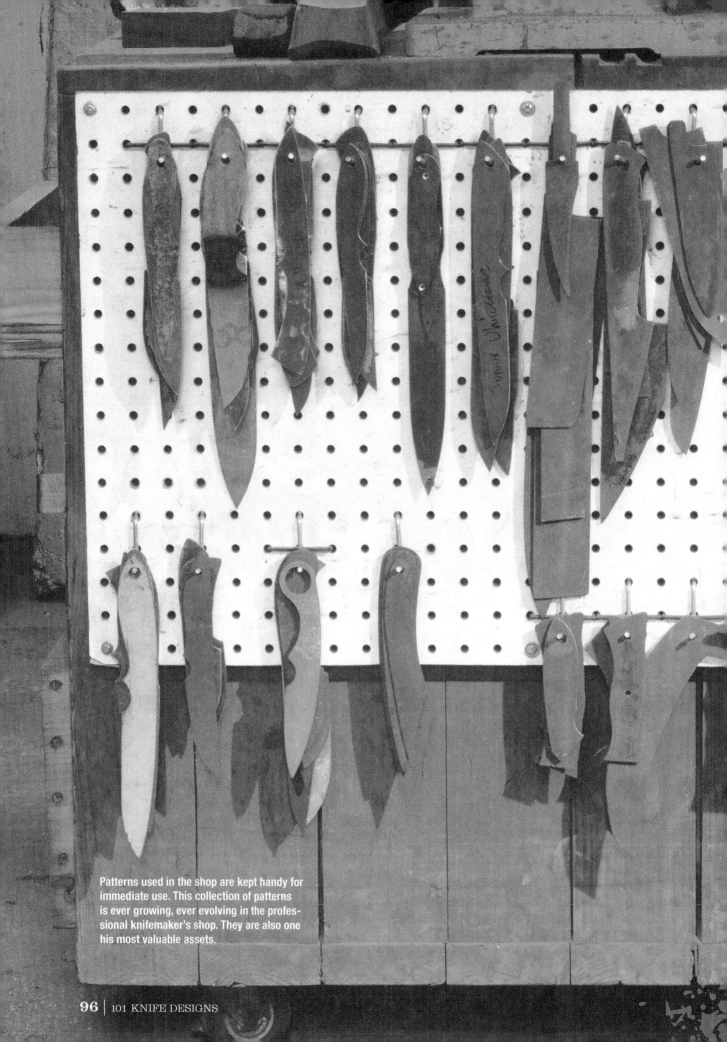

Patterns used in the shop are kept handy for immediate use. This collection of patterns is ever growing, ever evolving in the professional knifemaker's shop. They are also one of his most valuable assets.

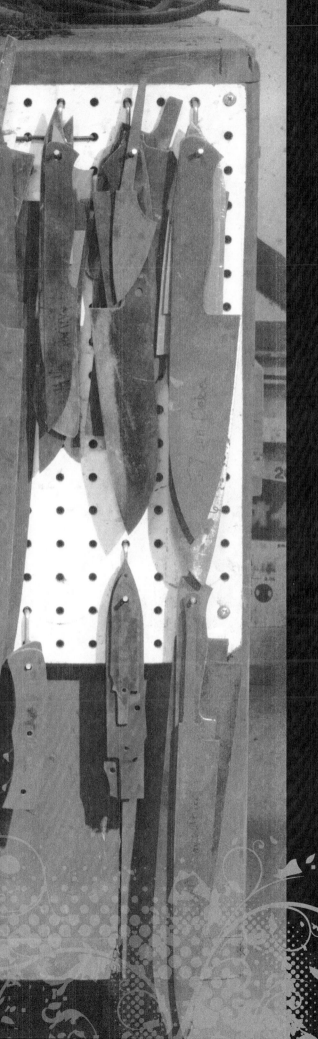

PART TWO

HOW TO CREATE AND PRESERVE NEW DESIGNS

If you have read this far, you know that knives need to be designed in terms of slicing, chopping or piercing. You also know that most practical knives fall into a useful size category. This book is full of useful patterns, many of which have proven to be great sellers over the years. The following procedure explains how I make a new pattern that can be used indefinitely.

STEP 1

I always start out with a new piece of photo copy paper and a pencil with a fine tip that is easy to erase. I lightly draw a line using a ruler lengthwise, and then I draw a line perpendicular somewhere along the first line to separate the handle from the blade.

STEP 2

With an idea in my head as to how the knife is going to be used in terms of slicing, chopping or piercing, I start to lightly sketch smooth flowing lines to establish the profile of the knife. I almost always make a smooth, uninterrupted line from the back of the blade to the handle, unless I am designing a dagger.

This is how they all start out. The cross lines are for reference and will be erased when the pattern profile is complete.

All blades except daggers and traditional Japanese kitchen knives have a smooth flowing profile from the spine of the knife to the handle.

As I sketch, I leave all the lines where they are because each of them, even ones that seem way off, is a reference for the line that I am trying to draw. If you erase all the lines you don't like immediately, you will get stuck.

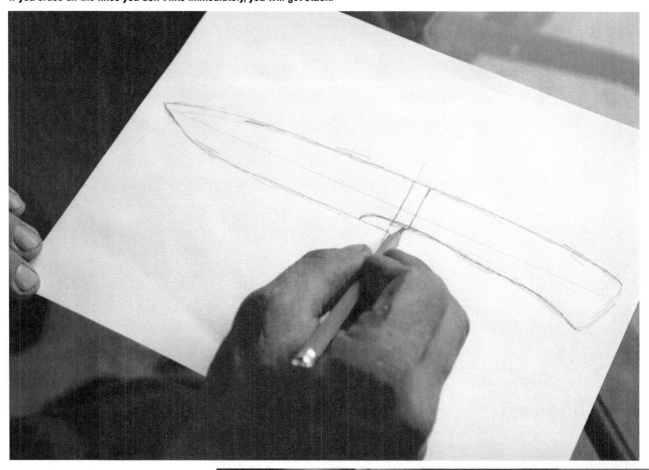

STEP 3

Once I can "see" the lines I like from among several light sketched lines, I trace them with a heavy pencil line. I check the profile lines by holding the piece of paper at eye level. Looking at the new pattern this way will reveal any high or low spots in the profile. I then erase all lines except the heavy pencil lines.

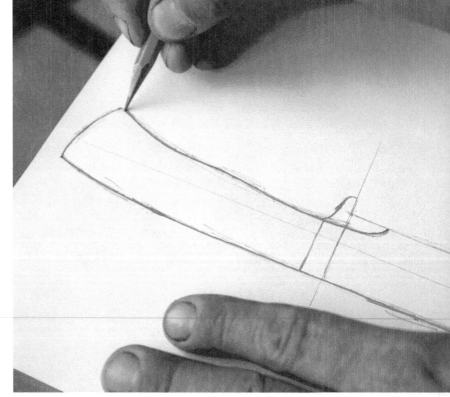

From the multitude of light sketches, I choose the best lines and go over them with heavy pencil.

If the heavy lines look right, I start to erase all the other sketch lines. (I also make sure to give the cute eraser back to my daughter when I'm done!).

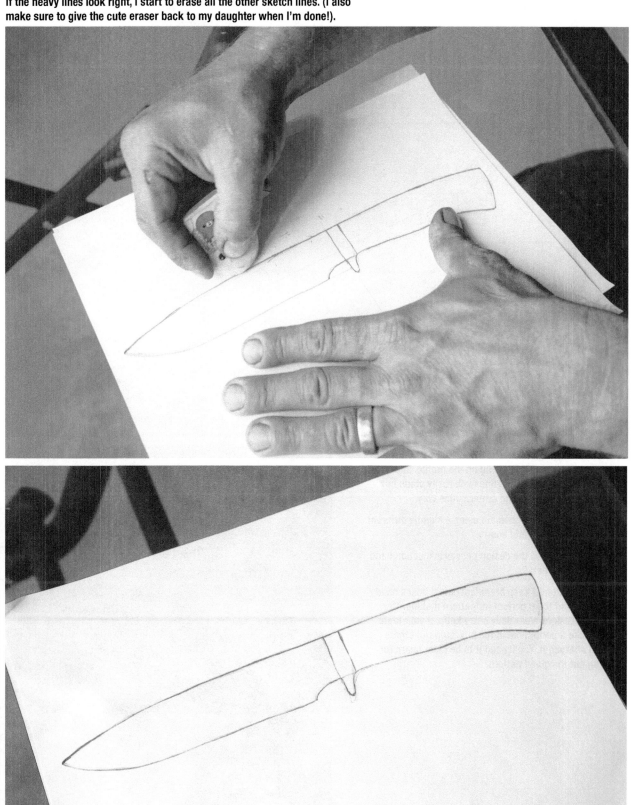

The original cross reference lines can now be erased.

(above) The design is checked from all angles by holding it at eye level and focusing on the profile. Subtle deviations from the profile lines will really stand out when holding designs and patterns this way.

(right) Check the design again using a slightly different angle and different light source.

(opposite top) Once the design passes inspection I add the blade grind details.

(opposite bottom) I keep breakfast cereal boxes handy because I find them perfect for pattern making. This is a great task for your daily carry knife. If your knife can't make a perfect cut in the box, stop right there and go sharpen it. You'll need it to be razor sharp for cutting out the glued pattern.

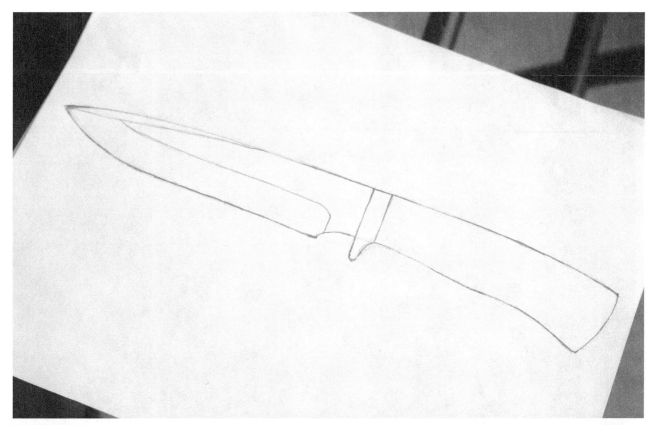

(left) Glue the pattern to the flat box. Don't glue over old creases in the box. Make sure not to use so much glue that the paper the pattern is on gets soaked. That will cause the pattern to distort.

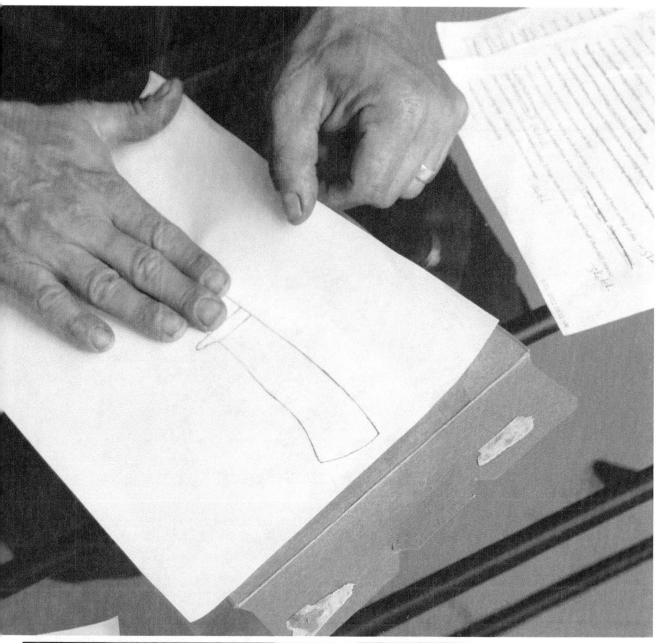

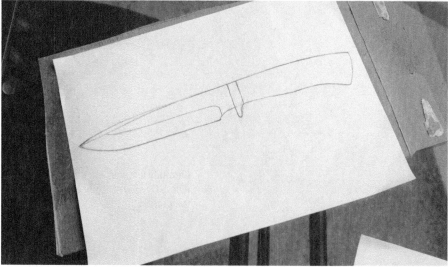

(above) Glue the pattern carefully. Visually confirm the pattern is straight.

(left) Give the pattern ample time to dry. (Hint, glue sticks dry the fastest, allowing you to cut out the pattern after ten minutes or so.)

Carefully use your razor sharp EDC
(Every Day Carry) knife to cut out
the pattern.

I like the knife better than scissors as it allows me to straighten out tiny imperfections in the line if there are any. (Hint, use the curved portion of your blade for long gentle curves and raise up to use the tip as you approach tight corners.)

(below) The cut out paper/cardboard pattern is held at eye level and examined from all angles.

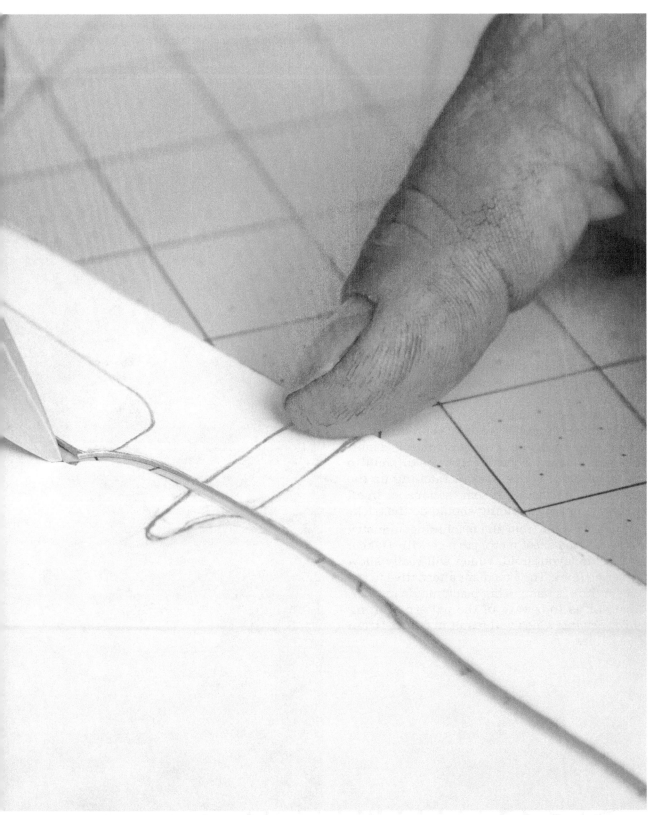

Done with the cut-out, but keep the borders in case you need them for reference later. If you lose your pattern, you could use the borders to reproduce it.

STEP 4

Once the pattern is drawn to my satisfaction, I glue the paper to cardboard, such as that used in cereal boxes. When the glue dries the pattern is carefully cut out with a sharp utility knife. Even if the design includes a guard, only the profile of the steel is cut out. If the design is a hidden tang knife, only the blade with tang is cut out. The cut pattern is once again held at eye level, from all different angles to confirm the desired shape. Adjustments can be made with an abrasive when necessary.

STEP 5

The paper/cardboard pattern must now be transferred to thin, flat sheet metal. While copper, tin, aluminum and other softer metals could be used, I prefer to use steel because it is the most durable around other hot steel. The pattern is securely held in place and traced with a metal scribe. If the sheet metal has unidirectional scratches on it, like is common on rolled steel or old hand saw blades, it might be difficult to clearly see your scribe lines. Scratching up the sheet metal surface with some sandpaper in all directions prior to scribing should do the trick.

Another trick from the machining industry is to paint the sheet metal surface with Dykem brand blue layout fluid, which will really show the scribe lines. The expedient alternative to the Dykem fluid is using a big black magic marker. A caution is to beware of the pattern shifting while scribing which will result in double "train track" lines.

Various scribes for transferring patterns to metal. The one thing they all have in common is they have fine sharp tips that are much harder than the metal they scribe. My favorite is a broken utility knife.

(above) Using a scribe, carefully trace the paper/cardboard pattern onto thin sheet metal.

(left) Sources of thin sheet metal for making patterns. Be sure to make patterns out of metal if you are a bladesmith working with and around hot steel. A stock removal knifemaker might get away with using a durable synthetic.

Some cold-rolled metal and old saw blades have unidirectional lines on them making it difficult to see the scribe lines that run parallel to them.

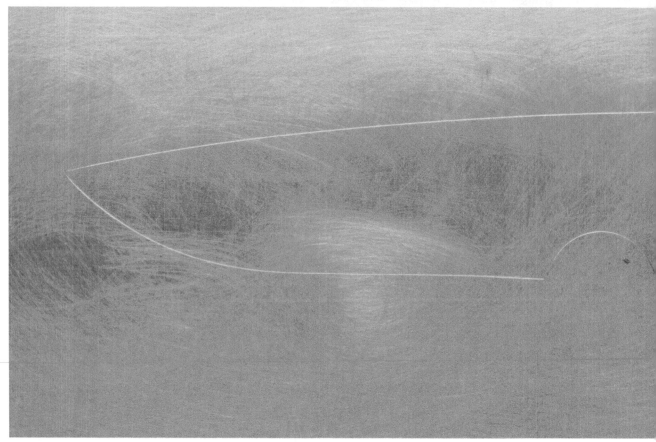

(above) Beware of the pattern shifting when scribing or else you might end up with double scribe lines. If this happens, you have two choices: 1) cut the pattern out to the inner lines, which makes a smaller knife or 2) polish the surface of the metal and scribe again.

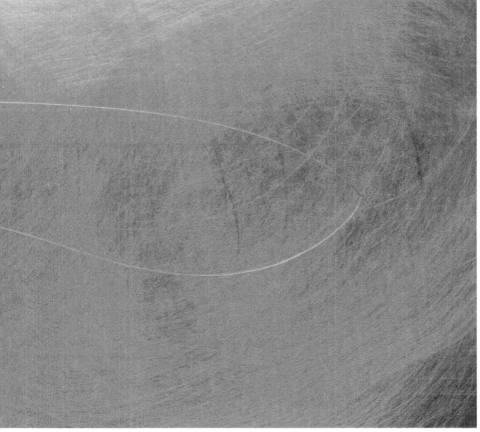

(left) One solution is to scratch up the surface with sandpaper. Keep in mind that this may affect your surface finish in the finished knife.

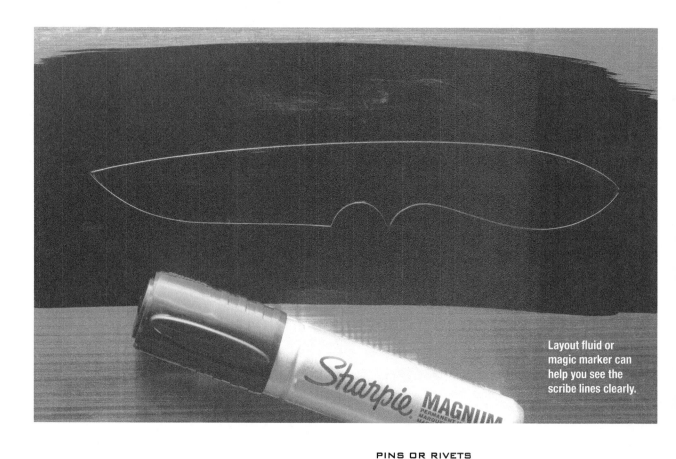

Layout fluid or magic marker can help you see the scribe lines clearly.

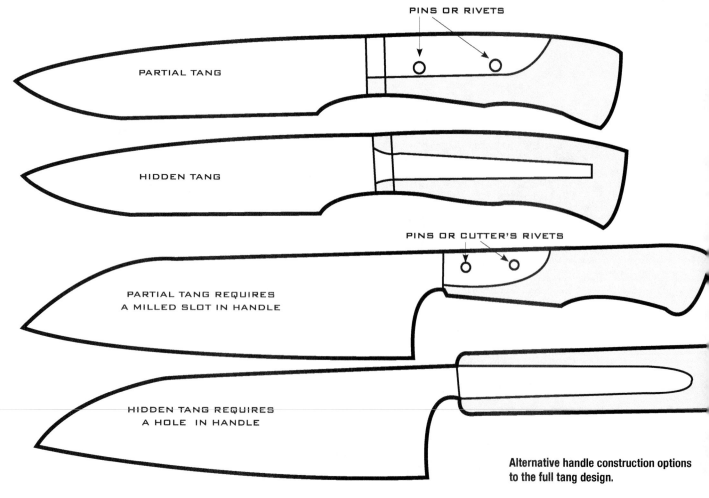

PINS OR RIVETS

PARTIAL TANG

HIDDEN TANG

PINS OR CUTTER'S RIVETS

PARTIAL TANG REQUIRES A MILLED SLOT IN HANDLE

HIDDEN TANG REQUIRES A HOLE IN HANDLE

Alternative handle construction options to the full tang design.

STEP 6

Cut out the pattern using whatever means you have at your disposal. I use a circular cut off wheel (chop saw), but other methods include a hack saw, band saw, drill press, grinder etc. Be sure to stay outside the scribe lines or you will end up with something different than what you designed. I then take as much time as nec-

Cutting out patterns with the circular chop saw. Notice the safety gear.

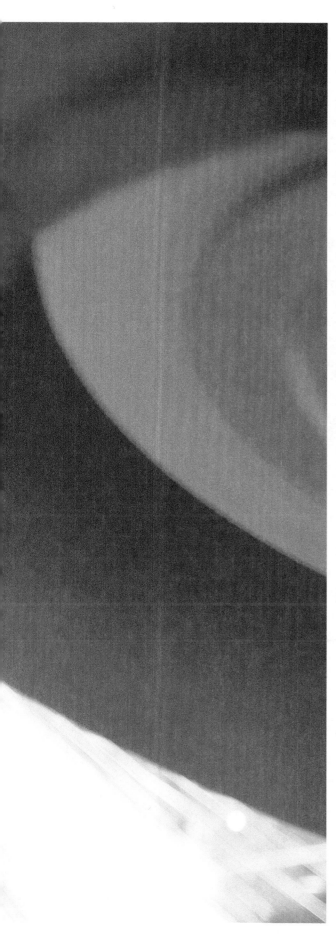

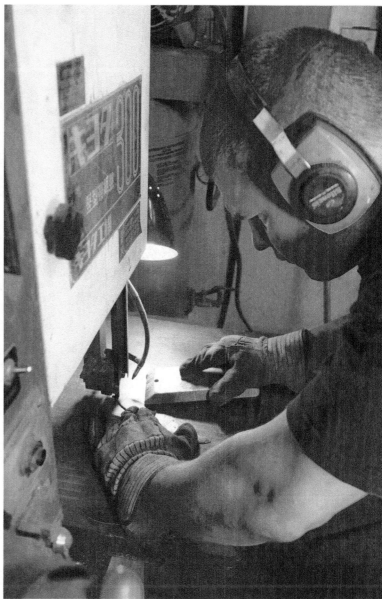

(above) Cutting out patterns on my band saw. Always use a push stick on the band saw.

(left) Easy does it with this machine; it left its mark on me a few times in my youth.

essary to grind the new pattern down to the scribe lines to exactly the shape I want. I will repeatedly hold the paper pattern over the metal pattern to verify my lines. I am constantly holding the pattern at eye level, in a good source of natural light, to check for high and low spots in the profile. This new pattern might be my next best seller, and as such it needs to be an absolutely perfect representation of the design. Treat this step as the most important in pattern development, because the collection of successful patterns is the most valuable physical asset a knifemaker has.

(above) A cloudy day is the best source of natural light to really examine the lines of knives.

(left) Notice the gate on the band saw is just high enough to clear the material being cut. This minimizes the risk of being injured if something slips.

Once I am satisfied with the lines of the pattern, I lightly sand the corners of the edges just enough to remove any burrs and to make the pattern friendly to my hand. I am careful not to sand too aggressively, which might alter the pattern's profile. I then drill a hole in the pattern at one end or another so I can hang it from a nail with all the other patterns. I suppose if you choose to store your patterns in a drawer or box, the drilled hole is not necessary.

(left) Sunny days can cast glare on shiny metal, making it difficult to micro-examine your knife.

(below) This is how I get all my profile lines exactly the way I want them with just my eyes...by careful micro-observation.

How to Grow Your Pattern Collection

It really is amazing to consider that when I started making neck knives 14 years ago I had just three patterns: the Original, the Wharncliffe and the Combat models. Now I have over forty neck knife patterns. A few of those were conceived on paper and transferred to sheet metal, but most of them are modifications of existing patterns.

It is my practice to forge knives in batches of between 20 and 100, depending on the style and complexity of the knife. In some cases I forge 20 neck knives and scribe them all for one pattern, say for example, the Original model. When cutting and grinding them out, I will purposely cut some lines short and leave other lines proud, in the spirit of experimentation. Then I lay them all out on a table or the clean floor (clean floor? Those of you who have been to my shop, stop laughing!) and look at them all together as a group. Inevitably, one of the cut out blades will stand out as being "just right." It is hard to imagine that less than half a millimeter can make that much difference, but it really does. At this point I immediately trace that blade onto another piece of sheet metal and make a new pattern. In fact, any time an experimental knife turns out great, I immediately trace it on sheet metal to make a new pattern. Several times in the past I have neglected to make a new pattern from a great knife and

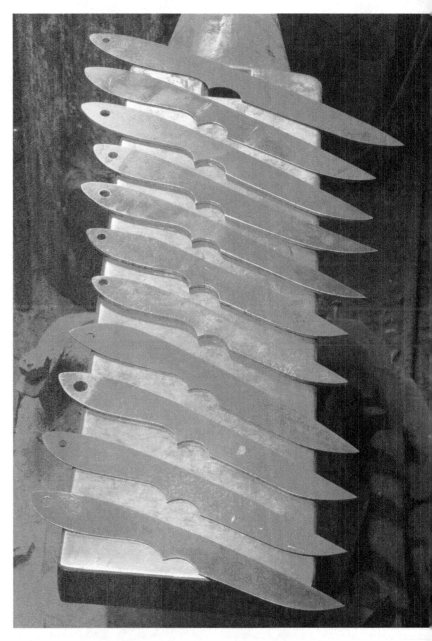

Ten patterns evolved from the Original neck knife. Each new pattern is slightly different from the Original, but yet unique enough to be worthy of its own name.

regretted it. You think to yourself at the time "I can reproduce that from memory," but some of the extremely subtle nuances in a blade design can be elusive to reproduce.

Another thing I often do for fun and profit is stretch a knife in various directions before heat-treating using a hammer. This hammering has the additional benefit of cold-forging the steel, but care must be taken not to overdo it because steel can crack from overworking. As a general rule, hammering the cutting edge of a blade curves the blade up like a slicing knife and hammering the spine of the blade causes the blade to curve down like a kopis design. If one of these modified patterns catches my eye, I immediately stop to make a pattern of it in sheet steel. Old, unpopular patterns can sometimes be given a "face-lift" through this cold forging technique.

Another view of the evolution of the
author's neck knife pattern collection.

How to Modify a Pattern to Improve It

With each new pattern I make, I get better and better at capturing the important nuances of practical blade design. New knife models at Carter Cutlery are met by customers with terrific enthusiasm. Some of my older, less useful patterns sit and collect dust, and eventually I will either recycle them or modify them with the intention of improving them by applying the better understanding I have gained through the years. Sometimes all that is necessary is a little cold forging and judicious grinding to bring an old pattern back to life.

(above) Three blades start out exactly the same size and shape.

(left) In about five seconds of cold forging the author radically changes the shapes of the blades.

The right blade is untouched and its spear-point shape is ideal for piercing. The middle blade was cold forged along the cutting edge resulting in a blade ideal for slicing. The left blade was cold forged along the spine (assuming there was enough material there to start with) which resulted in a blade suggestive of the Kopis design, which is a chopper.

(above) Old knife patterns that no longer make the cut. They can be recycled or perhaps modified for success.

(right) A bit of stretching under the hammer here and there…

This old pattern might have some potential for improvement. I think I can see a good blade in there waiting to come out!

...looking better, but not quite there...

...Ah! That's more like it.

...I can feel it moving under the power of the blows...

(above) Now I refine the blade to look like my popular Clave model neck knife...

(right) ...checking the profile in the light to make sure it is the way I want it and...

...enlarging the choil to a useful size
and shaping up the handle...

...Voila! A successful facelift for an old pattern.

Specific Features of Blades

Point Location and Sharpness

If you intend for a knife to have good piercing ability, the point should line up somewhere near the center of the blade, and the blade should be in line with the handle, which is where the thrusting power comes from. Consider the armor from centuries past. Many of the helmets and breastplates had ridges to deflect the blow of edges weapons. Anything less than a 90-degree strike to the armor would be deflected. Likewise, the most effective piercing occurs when the force from the hand, the blade and the point are all aligned. A narrow and thin blade pierces better because it has less surface area. Finally, the point has to be brought to a "thumbtack sharp" point when given the final sharpening at completion.

During the early years at my knife shop in Tabaruzaka, Kumamoto, Japan, I had written on my shop walls in plain view, "Get the point!" to encourage and remind me to put a "thumbtack sharp" point on every knife I sold.

POINT HIGH OF CENTER;
SUGGESTS BLADE IS FOR SLICING.

POINT AT OR NEAR CENTER;
SUGGESTS BLADE IS FOR PIERCCING.

POINT LOW OF CENTER;
SUGGESTS BLADE IS FOR CHOPPING.

The position of the point in relation to the center of the blade suggests the intended use of the blade – slicing, piercing or chopping.

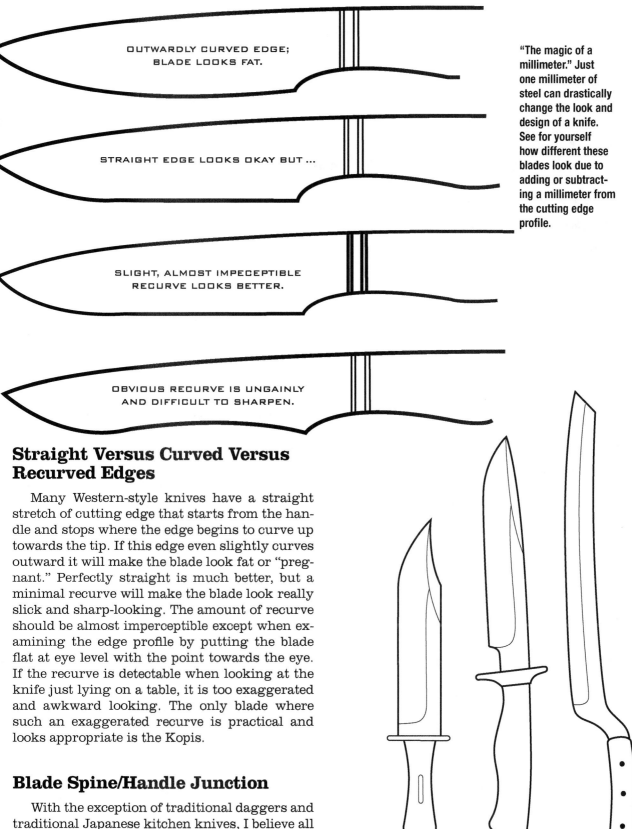

OUTWARDLY CURVED EDGE;
BLADE LOOKS FAT.

STRAIGHT EDGE LOOKS OKAY BUT ...

SLIGHT, ALMOST IMPECEPTIBLE
RECURVE LOOKS BETTER.

OBVIOUS RECURVE IS UNGAINLY
AND DIFFICULT TO SHARPEN.

"The magic of a millimeter." Just one millimeter of steel can drastically change the look and design of a knife. See for yourself how different these blades look due to adding or subtracting a millimeter from the cutting edge profile.

Straight Versus Curved Versus Recurved Edges

Many Western-style knives have a straight stretch of cutting edge that starts from the handle and stops where the edge begins to curve up towards the tip. If this edge even slightly curves outward it will make the blade look fat or "pregnant." Perfectly straight is much better, but a minimal recurve will make the blade look really slick and sharp-looking. The amount of recurve should be almost imperceptible except when examining the edge profile by putting the blade flat at eye level with the point towards the eye. If the recurve is detectable when looking at the knife just lying on a table, it is too exaggerated and awkward looking. The only blade where such an exaggerated recurve is practical and looks appropriate is the Kopis.

Blade Spine/Handle Junction

With the exception of traditional daggers and traditional Japanese kitchen knives, I believe all knives look and function best when the transition from the blade to the handle is in line with the spine of the blade. Likewise, any knife designed with a main purpose other than piercing should not have a guard that rises above the back of the knife. Such a guard severely limits the way the knife can be held in the hand.

These three examples leave a lot to be desired. The knife on the right offers a solution to a problem that doesn't exist. The Bowie knife (left) ends up with a mismatched handle because the maker got carried away with the blade. The last example (center) illustrates how an otherwise-useful design is spoiled by a guard that extends past the spine of the blade.

Those Ridiculous Tanto Points

I know this is going to step on a lot of people's toes, but it needs to be said: tanto points are useless. Hear me out – I know you will agree with me once you read my explanation. And please remember, my goal here is to educate on practical knife design, and not to disrespect the makers of exotic blades.

Despite what you have been told, tanto points do not make a point any stronger for piercing. Any strength that is in the point comes from the thickness of the metal right behind the tip of the blade, and is not dependent on the blade profile. What you have not been told by the tanto point salesman though, is that the very same tanto point will impede good piercing because of the extra drag produced by the protrusion of the square point.

Furthermore, we have established that the function of utility knives with blades less than four inches is slicing, with some superficial piercing required from time to time. As slicing knives, short blades are mostly limited by their blade length. A tanto point blade further limits the slicing ability by dividing a short blade into two smaller blades, divided by an angle. You have just cut the slicing power of a small knife in two! What's more, because the second angled tanto edge sticks out from the blade profile, in use it is the first part to go dull. (Go ahead, check your tanto knives that have seen a few hours of use. You will see a shiny spot right on that corner when held edge up in a good source of light!) So now, when you try to make a slicing cut, you are leading the cut with a dull edge.

Now this third point is painfully obvious to any tanto blade owner who ever tried to sharpen his knife; tanto blades are difficult to sharpen. It really is as difficult as sharpening two small blades at one time.

But, you say, if the tanto point isn't functional, then why is it featured on the world's most famous blade of all time, the Japanese Samurai sword? Well, I'm glad you asked. The kissaki, or tanto point, became popular during times of relative peace within feudal Japan, when Katana were admired more for their intrinsic beauty than for their practicality in battle. These sword points were costly to manufacture, costly to have sharpened and polished and would render a sword useless once the hardened steel was sharpened away. I assure you that many swords in Japan that actually saw continuous use in battles had curved tips (like the reground folding knife picture here). Some of these swords have survived to be included in museums, but many of these desirable blades were used up over decades until they were no longer useful, then probably reforged into new tools. Again, I'll mention that the common tendency is for the less useful blades to survive in pristine condition and make it into museums. Remember what the most prestigious Japanese Temple carpenters (Miya Daiku) say, that the best blades get used up and never make it to the second-hand store.

So why, pray tell, are these blades so popular? The answer lies in successful marketing that capitalizes on consumer's desire for the new and exotic. The cutlery industry as a whole was in a funk back in the beginning of the 1980s. Manu-

Common commercially sold tanto point knife (... sigh of frustration...).

Simple and quick regrind removing the tanto point and thus greatly improving the functionality of the blade. This, I assure you, comes with no loss of point strength and pierces easier too. Easier to use, easier to sharpen, slices way better and looks practical to boot.

facturers were offering the same knife models that they had for decades and, frankly, consumers were hungry for something new. The new company Cold Steel, under the leadership of pioneer Lynn Thompson, introduced the American version of the Japanese tanto, and they sold like hot cakes. You may wonder just how many of those knives were ever used on a day-to-day basis. Based on my understanding of practical cutlery, I'd say very few. But that didn't matter to the millions of customers who bought them. The same phenomenon occurred with other exotic blades, such as the flat-backed (incorrect design) chisel

grind blades, the karambit knives, radically recurved blades, the Tom Brown Tracker (pound for pound, the most useless knife that can't even be improved by regrinding) and recently, knives with radically bent handles in relation to the angle of the blade. Successful marketing does not equate with successful, practical knives!

Now, before you take me for a prude, let me say that I love capitalism and the free market. If you want to buy exotic knives, good on you and good for the economy. Now at least you won't be under the impression that you are buying a practical knife.

Handle Shape, Contour and Angle Relative to the Blade

The handle has two functions: to transfer the human input to the cutting edge of the blade and to naturally index the cutting edge with the direction of knife movement. Straight oval handles are appropriate for daggers and most kitchen knives, but slightly downward curved handles with egg shaped oval contour excel on single edged knives. However, too much angle difference between blade and handle will impair control from the hand to the blade.

Knife handles should be smooth and free of any rough spots. Cutting grooves or adding checkering to a handle for a more secure grip will not only cause blisters during prolonged use, but will also present cleaning and maintenance difficulties. Likewise, in climates with big humidity changes throughout the year, handles that incorporate both natural materials with metal spacers should be avoided. Too often the natural material shrinks, leaving sharp or rough edges of the metal washers protruding. Using natural materials that have been chemically stabilized will minimize this problem.

Handle shapes that allow the hand to grip and hold it in many different configurations will see far more use than handles that lock the hand into one position. This is why knives with handles that have deep finger grooves, sub-hilts, D-guards and knuckle dusters don't lend themselves well to practical daily use.

You can almost see the flow of energy as this knife literally becomes an extension of Murray's hand.

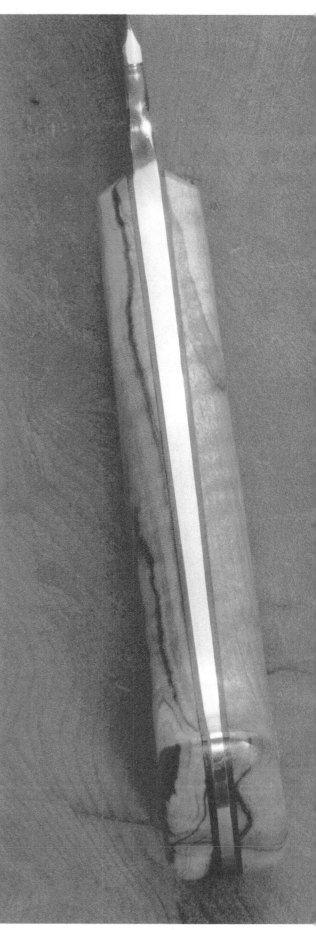

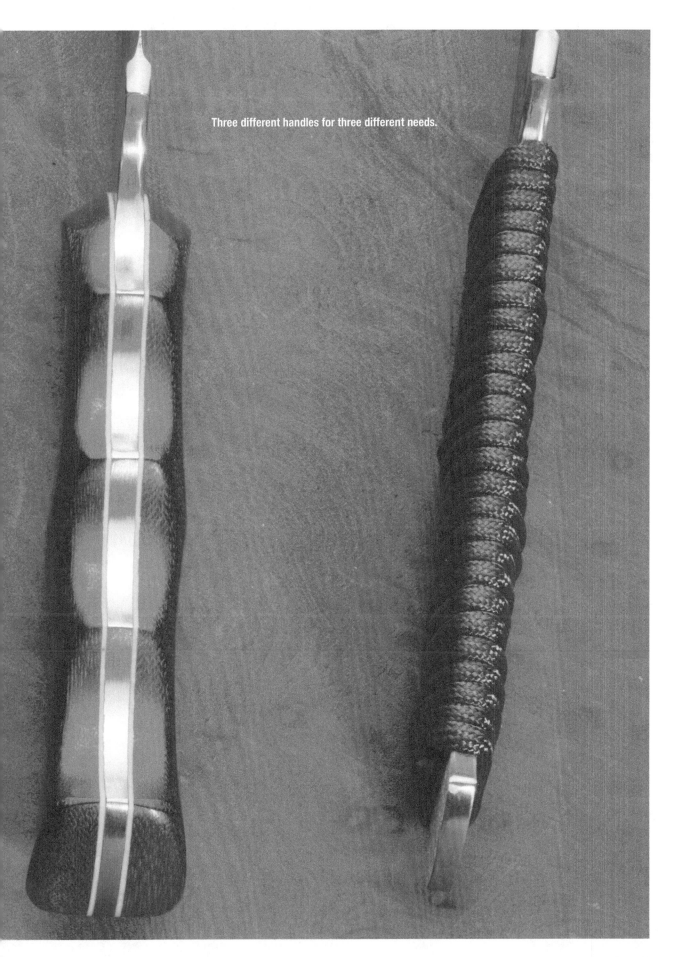

Three different handles for three different needs.

Three different handle options for the same knife: (left) olive wood scales with straight sides and no finger grooves, (middle) contoured black micarta scales with shallow finger grooves and (right) rope wrapped handle for thinness, lightweight and simplicity. This method of rope wrap can be re-wrapped in the field in less than five minutes.

(below) Straight handles have worked on kitchen knives for millennia.

(bottom) Power and control from the arm to the hand to the cutting edge of the knife depend on how smooth the flow of energy is, which depends on a correct handle angle for the knife and cutting task.

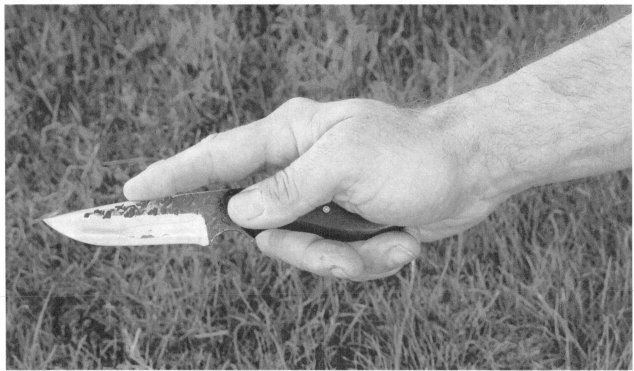

Low Drag, Easily-Maintained Profile

Knives should be absent of any feature that distracts from a smooth profile and that prevents easy cleaning and maintenance. Gut hooks, jimping, serrations, saw teeth and choils seriously compromise a blade's practicality.

There are two types of choils; Type 1 is a small semi-circle void where the cutting portion of the blade starts, and Type 2 choils are the gap between the handle and the blade heel on a wide bladed knife.

Finger choils; if there is to be a choil on a knife, let it serve a purpose. The top and bottom examples are too short and too long and serve no function.

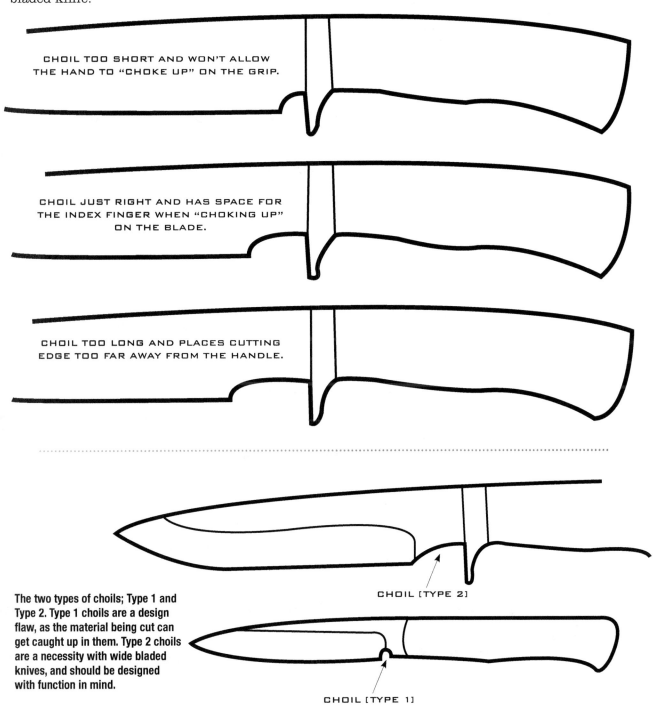

CHOIL TOO SHORT AND WON'T ALLOW THE HAND TO "CHOKE UP" ON THE GRIP.

CHOIL JUST RIGHT AND HAS SPACE FOR THE INDEX FINGER WHEN "CHOKING UP" ON THE BLADE.

CHOIL TOO LONG AND PLACES CUTTING EDGE TOO FAR AWAY FROM THE HANDLE.

CHOIL [TYPE 2]

The two types of choils; Type 1 and Type 2. Type 1 choils are a design flaw, as the material being cut can get caught up in them. Type 2 choils are a necessity with wide bladed knives, and should be designed with function in mind.

CHOIL [TYPE 1]

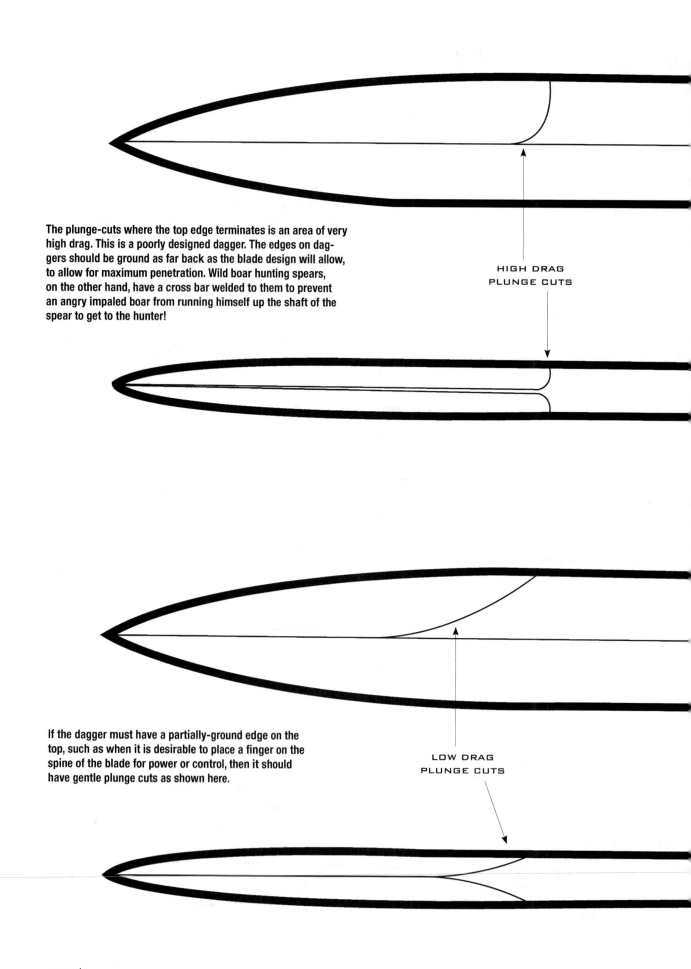

The plunge-cuts where the top edge terminates is an area of very high drag. This is a poorly designed dagger. The edges on daggers should be ground as far back as the blade design will allow, to allow for maximum penetration. Wild boar hunting spears, on the other hand, have a cross bar welded to them to prevent an angry impaled boar from running himself up the shaft of the spear to get to the hunter!

HIGH DRAG
PLUNGE CUTS

If the dagger must have a partially-ground edge on the top, such as when it is desirable to place a finger on the spine of the blade for power or control, then it should have gentle plunge cuts as shown here.

LOW DRAG
PLUNGE CUTS

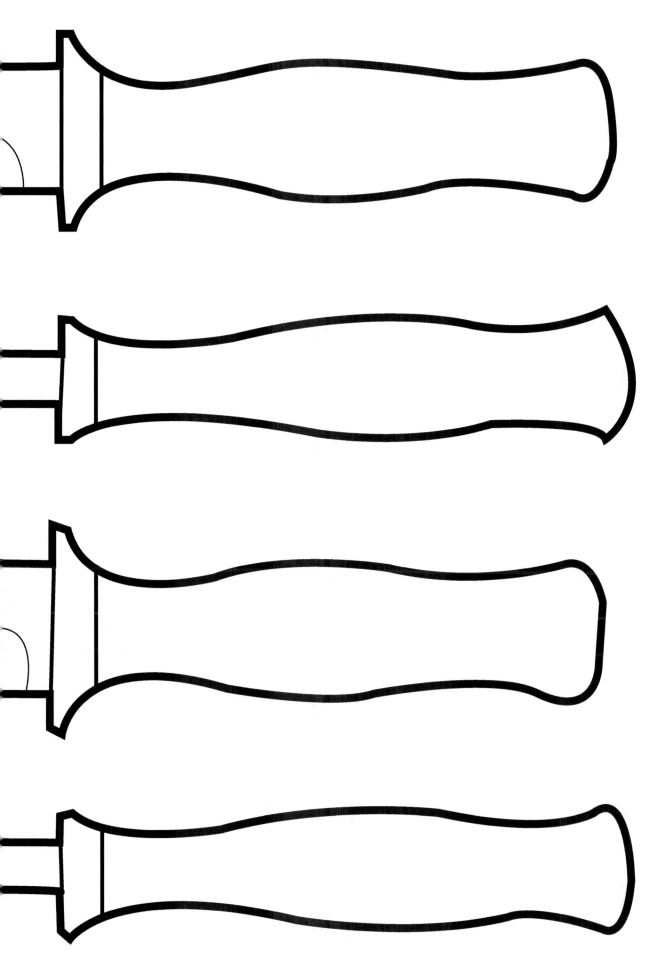

(left) A common factory knife with a gut hook marketed to hunters, for expedient evisceration. The theory is sound, but maintenance is problematic.

(below) Shallow filed grooves in the blade profile are called jimping. This is supposed to help the user keep a grip on the knife when the hands are wet, bloody or greasy. Actually, they just add an element of higher maintenance to the knife without offering any real advantage. A properly designed handle will provide all the gripping surface necessary, even in adverse conditions.

Sharp Pommels

There should not be any sharp protrusions from the end of the handle, as it will limit the number of ways the knife can be held and used.

The 89 Degree Subtlety

When designing knives with guards, follow the 89 degree rule. Favor the guard angle by just one degree by angling the top of the guard slightly towards the blade. The result will be an almost imperceptible difference that will improve the look of the knife. Likewise, when designing traditional Japanese kitchen knives, angle the heel of the blade back just one degree for a proper aesthetic look. Don't overdo it because these improvements look best when they are barely perceptible. You are actually appealing to the subconscious.

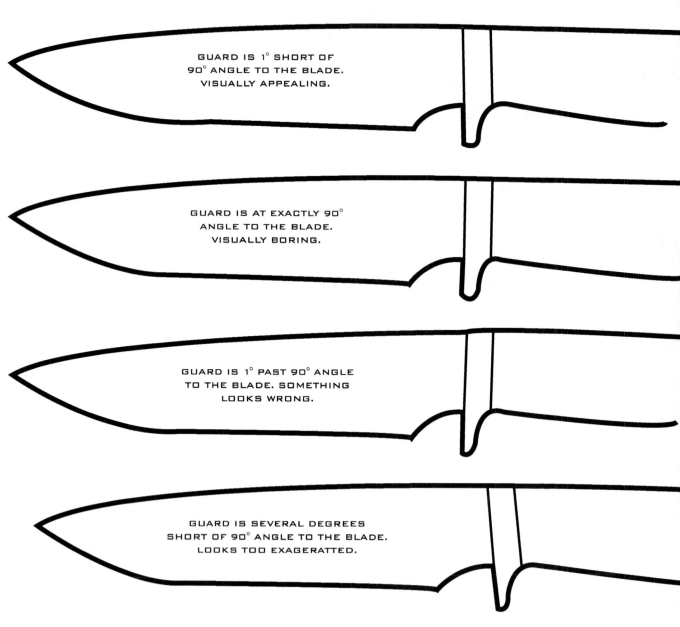

GUARD IS 1° SHORT OF
90° ANGLE TO THE BLADE.
VISUALLY APPEALING.

GUARD IS AT EXACTLY 90°
ANGLE TO THE BLADE.
VISUALLY BORING.

GUARD IS 1° PAST 90° ANGLE
TO THE BLADE. SOMETHING
LOOKS WRONG.

GUARD IS SEVERAL DEGREES
SHORT OF 90° ANGLE TO THE BLADE.
LOOKS TOO EXAGERATTED.

**The 89 degree rule at work in knives.
Tilting the guard forward by one degree
radically improves the design.**

The 89 degree rule at work in kitchen knives.
Angling the heel of the blade one degree short
of 90 degrees looks perfect.

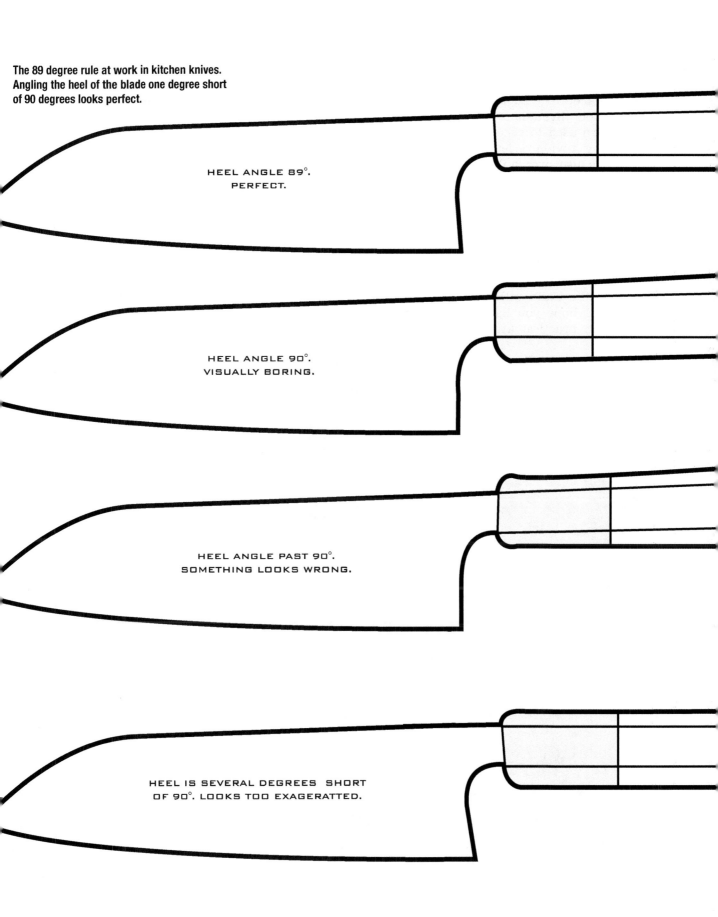

HEEL ANGLE 89°.
PERFECT.

HEEL ANGLE 90°.
VISUALLY BORING.

HEEL ANGLE PAST 90°.
SOMETHING LOOKS WRONG.

HEEL IS SEVERAL DEGREES SHORT
OF 90°. LOOKS TOO EXAGERATTED.

In an effort to identify the practical traits of common cutlery, I considered man's need of cutting tools throughout history in terms of how they are used to slice, chop and pierce. In examining a wide variety of blades that saw continuous use over millennia, we've definitively concluded that successful blades share many similar features, identified in this book.

If you are a knifemaker or bladesmith, I hope you have benefitted from the sharing of my knowledge, and that you enjoy financial benefits from applying this information or using my personal knife patterns for commerce.

For the knife enthusiast who has followed along, I hope you have enjoyed this journey through practical knife design and that you now have a much better understanding of desirable features in using knives.

I am confident that readers of all backgrounds are clear on how any particular knife they encounter will function in terms of how it will slice, chop or pierce.

Let me finish by stating that the ultimate value of any knife is not solely dependent on its inherent usefulness. Some knives have sentimental value and others serve to fulfill a need or desire in our heart. If you desire knives with features that I have demonstrated are not practical, by all means, exercise your God-given freedom and buy what you want. Not all knives in a collection have to be practical.

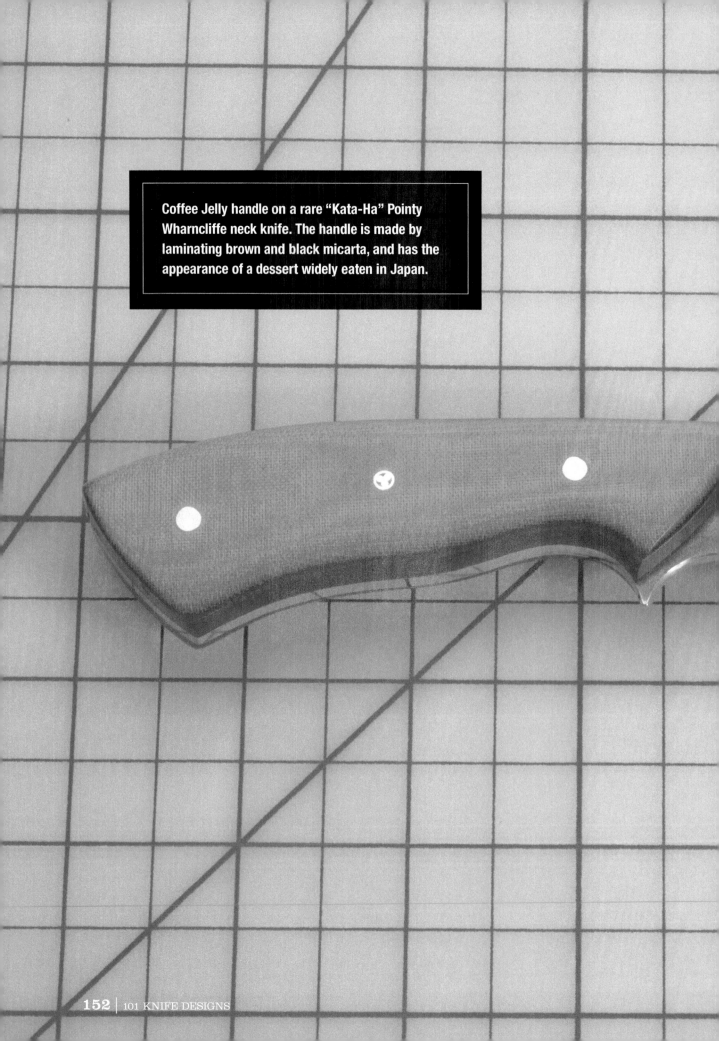

Coffee Jelly handle on a rare "Kata-Ha" Pointy Wharncliffe neck knife. The handle is made by laminating brown and black micarta, and has the appearance of a dessert widely eaten in Japan.

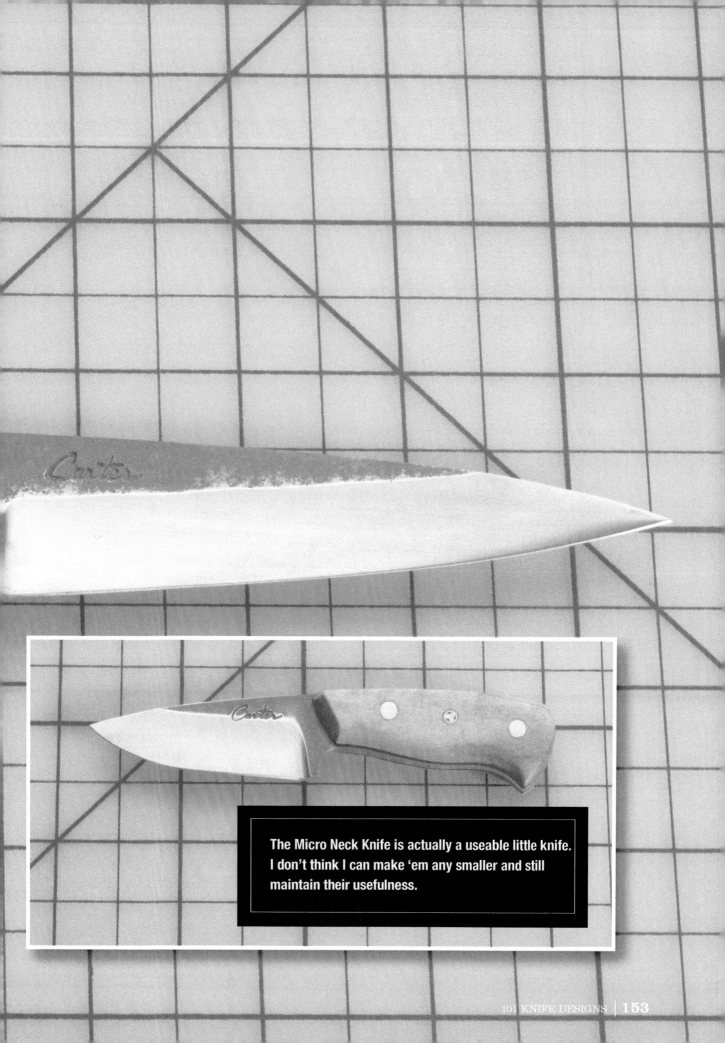

The Micro Neck Knife is actually a useable little knife.
I don't think I can make 'em any smaller and still
maintain their usefulness.

Slim Jim Neck Knife in ironwood. Notice the 50% reduced size "Carter" stamp used for smaller/narrower knives.

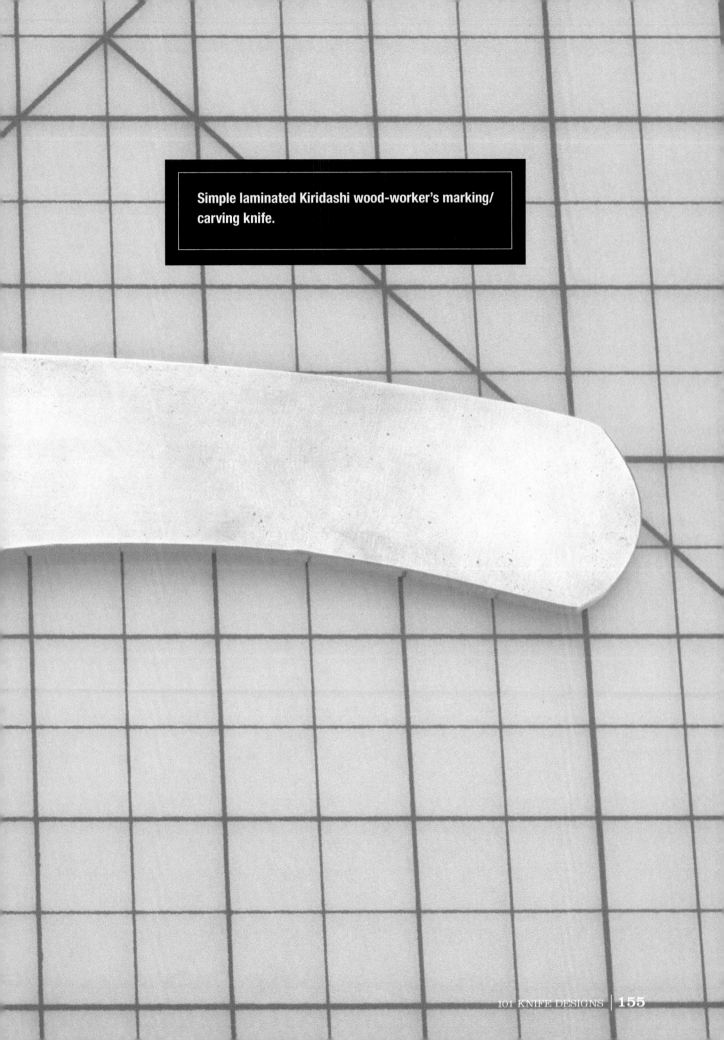

Simple laminated Kiridashi wood-worker's marking/
carving knife.

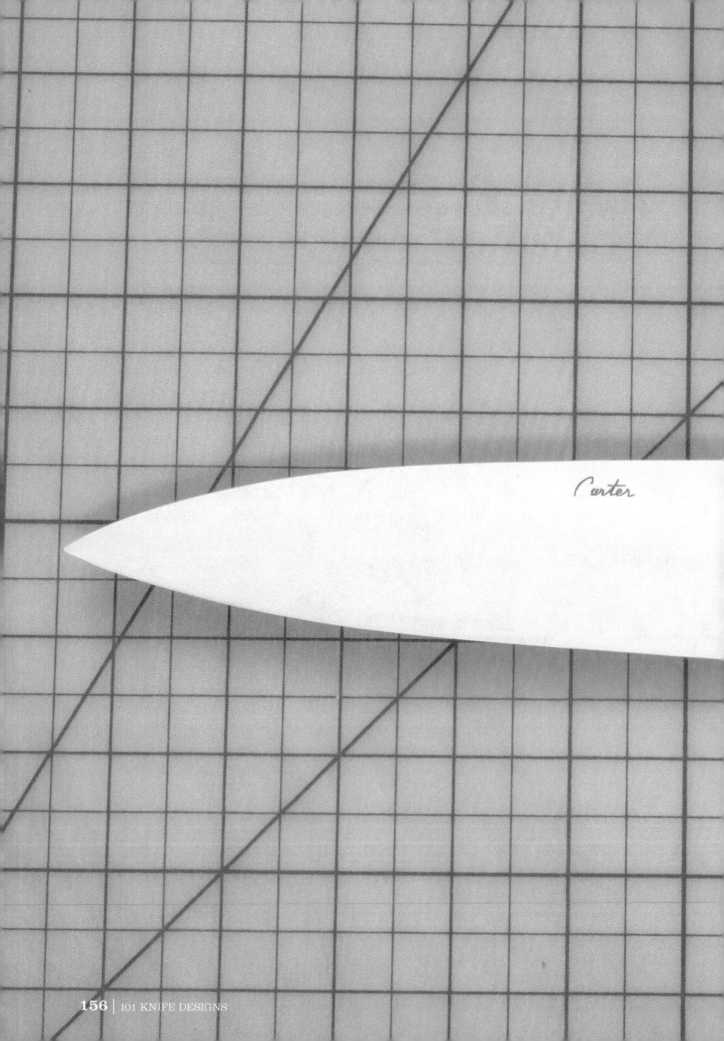

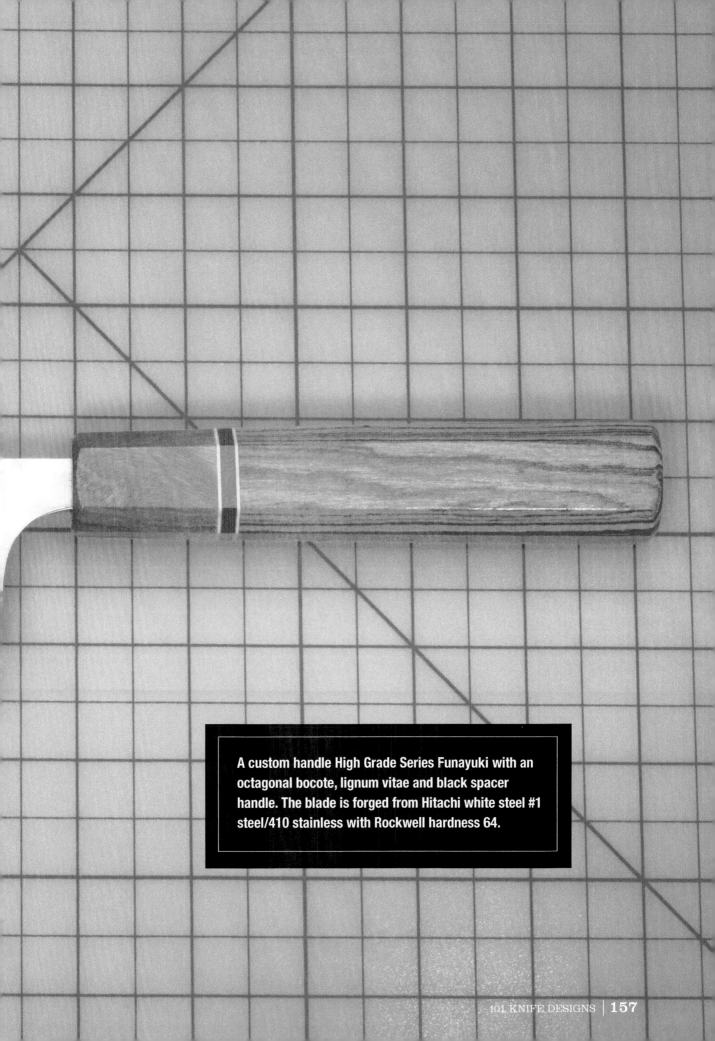

A custom handle High Grade Series Funayuki with an octagonal bocote, lignum vitae and black spacer handle. The blade is forged from Hitachi white steel #1 steel/410 stainless with Rockwell hardness 64.

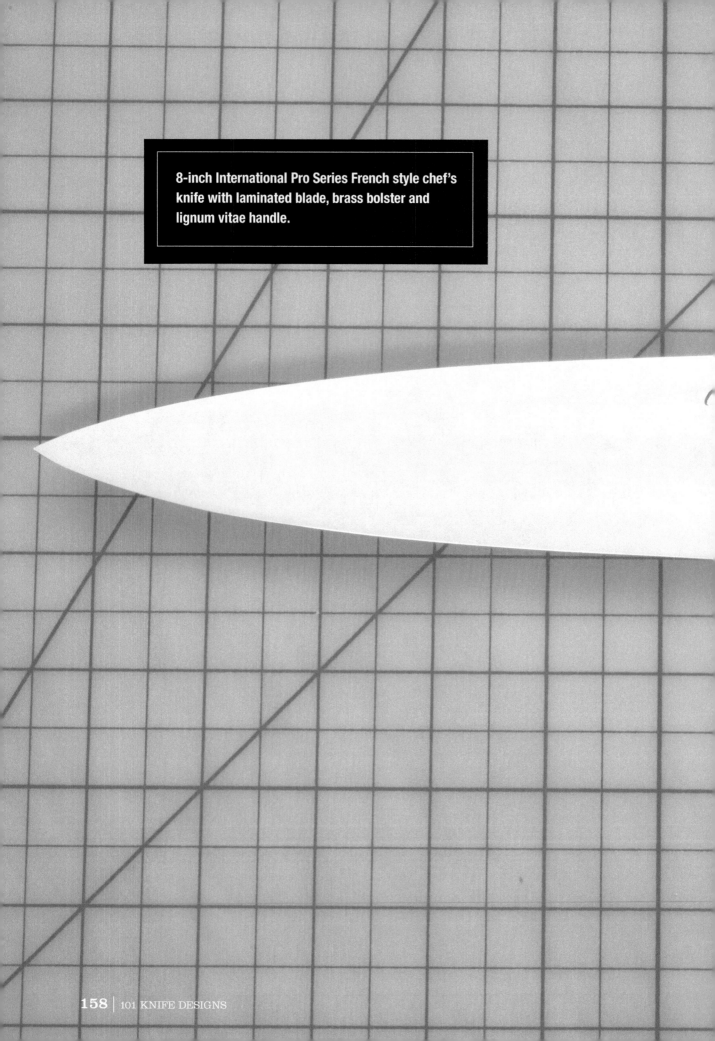

8-inch International Pro Series French style chef's knife with laminated blade, brass bolster and lignum vitae handle.

White Corian handled International Pro Series Kuro Uchi paring knife with brass bolster.

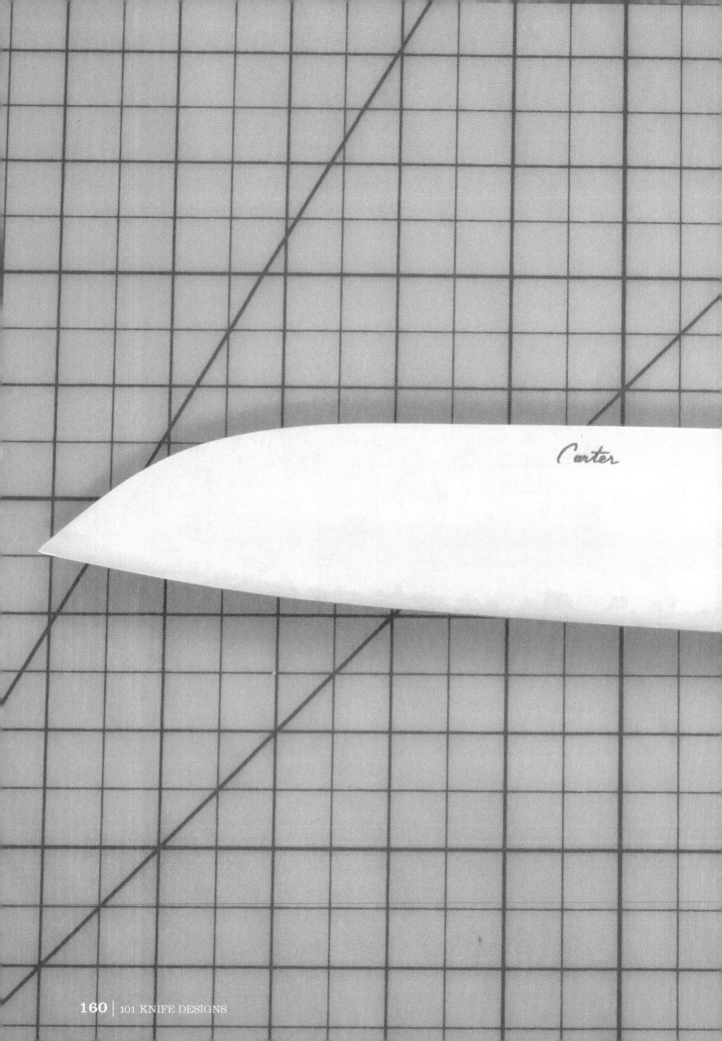

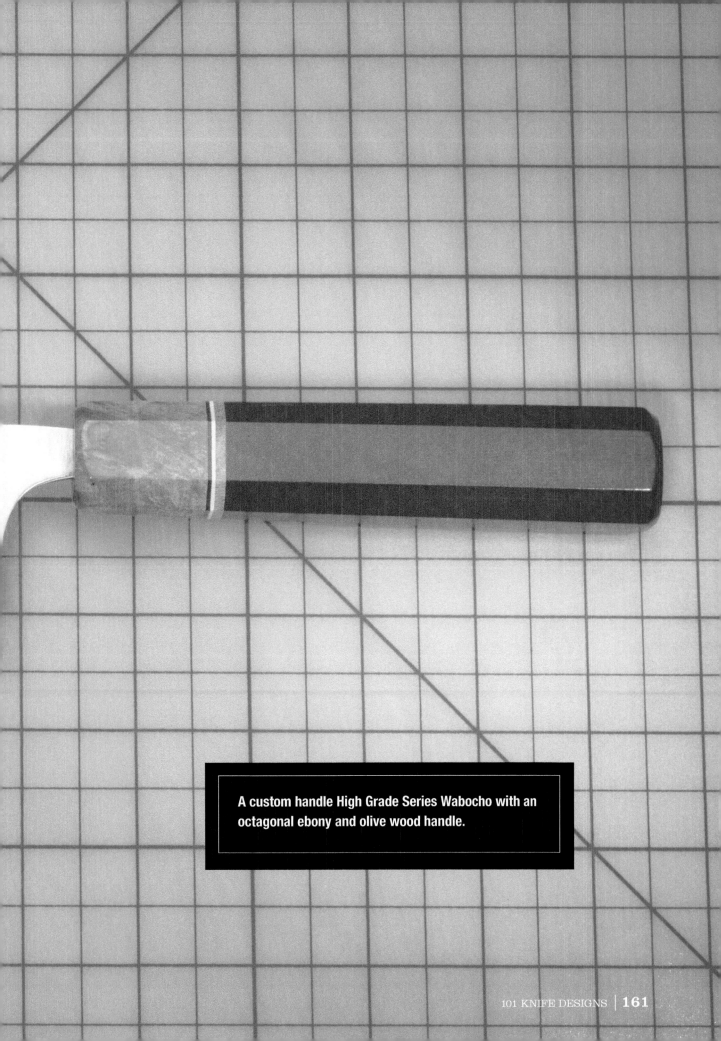

A custom handle High Grade Series Wabocho with an octagonal ebony and olive wood handle.

How to Use The Patterns

As the title implies, I have included 101 designs that I use in my shop. Many of these designs have allowed me to not only put food on the table for my wife and four children, but also to expand my business in many different directions. Many of these successful patterns have been stepping-stones to new successes. I hope they will do the same for you.

There are actually more than 101 patterns included, because many of them can be used in more than one way to create a new pattern. The daggers are two patterns in one because they are reversible. Some patterns, such as the kitchen knives, are of blades only, and can be paired up with either western handles or Japanese handles. Pictures of completed knives throughout the book can be used as reference and for inspiration. The illustration on page 114 shows how the partial tang and hidden tang knives can be paired with handles. Also, handles from one knife can be paired with a blade from another.

From This Book To Real Size

With the exception of a few of the larger patterns, most can be photocopied directly out of this book for use at 100%. The larger patterns have been reduced in size to fit in the book. Fol-

low the instructions within the pattern itself for copying to correct size (i.e. 133%, 200%, etc.). A pattern that says Enlarge 200%" will end up twice as big as it appears in the book. Your printer at home may not be able to print out the larger knives, at which point you might seek the services of specialty printing companies.

Please note that kitchen knife measurements are for the blade only and all other knives are measured from the tip of the blade to the heel of the handle.

The Dagger Designs

The dagger designs in particular are meant to give the user the choice between a recurved blade and a straight edged blade. You will notice that those patterns have two very small holes, one near the tip and one near the tang. After you transfer the paper pattern to cardboard, carefully drill the holes or punch them out with a small leather punch. Place the pattern directly on cardboard and put two small pencil marks where the holes are. Trace one side of the pattern. Now, flip the pattern over and line up the holes with the pencil marks. Trace the other side for a perfectly symmetrical pattern.

KNIFE PATTERNS/ TEMPLATES

PLEASE NOTE THAT KITCHEN KNIFE MEASUREMENTS ARE FOR
THE BLADE ONLY AND ALL OTHER KNIVES ARE MEASURED FROM
THE TIP OF THE BLADE TO THE HEEL OF THE HANDLE.

ALL THE FOLLOWING PATTERNS SHARE A COMMON METRIC
MEASUREMENT IN MILLIMETERS (MM), HOWEVER, THE
WESTERN PATTERNS START WITH AN INCH MEASUREMENT
AND THE JAPANESE PATTERNS START WITH A "SUN"
MEASUREMENT. ONE JAPANESE SUN IS APPROXIMATELY
1.2 INCHES (5 SUN = APPROX. 6 INCHES).

4.05 INCH / 103MM PARING KNIFE

3.25 INCH / 82MM PARING KNIFE

4.25 INCH / 108MM PARING KNIFE

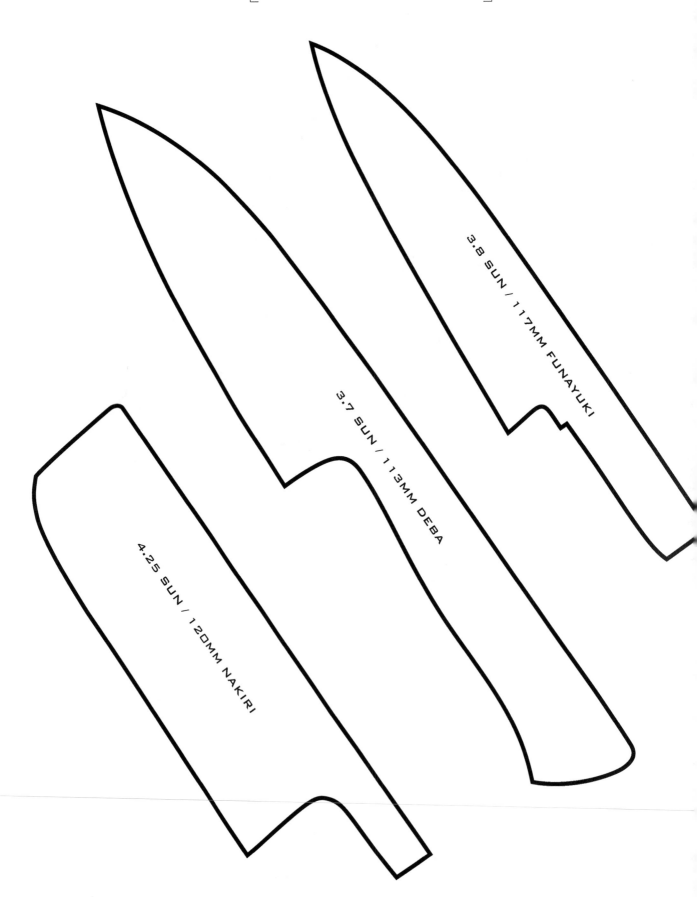

3.8 SUN / 117MM FUNAYUKI

3.7 SUN / 113MM DEBA

4.25 SUN / 120MM NAKIRI

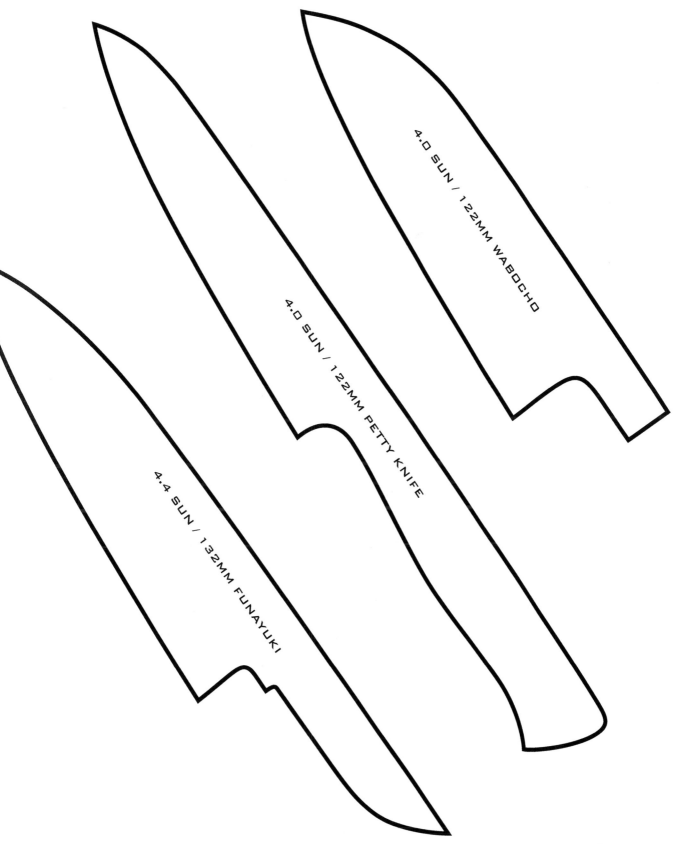

4.0 SUN / 122MM WABOCHO

4.0 SUN / 122MM PETTY KNIFE

4.4 SUN / 132MM FUNAYUKI

4.6 SUN / 140MM HONESUKI

5.5 INCH / 137MM PREP KNIFE

4.5 SUN / 138MM HONESUKI

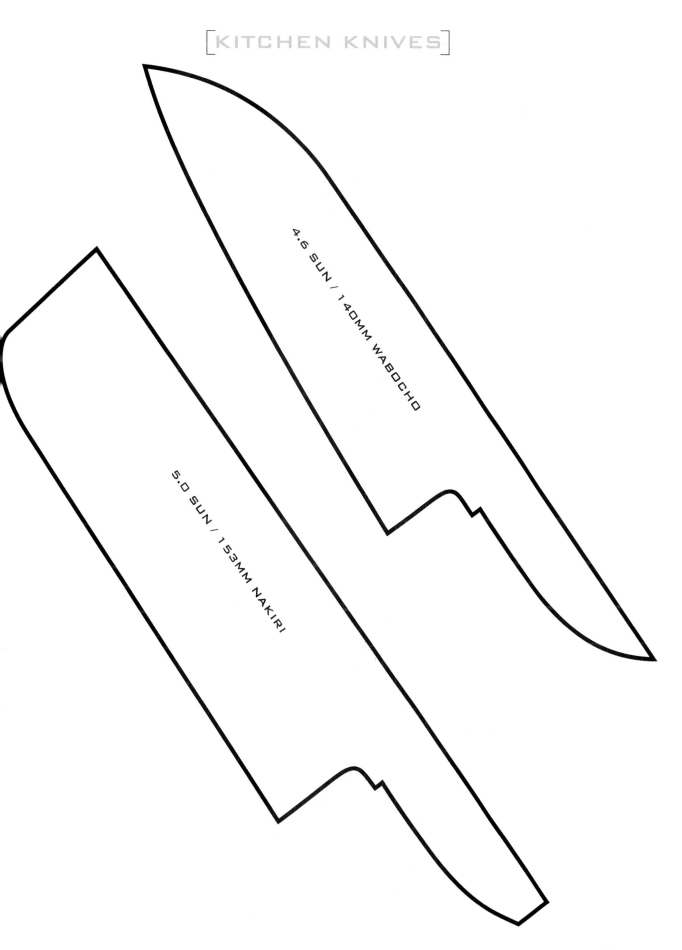

4.6 SUN / 140MM WABOCHO

5.0 SUN / 153MM NAKIRI

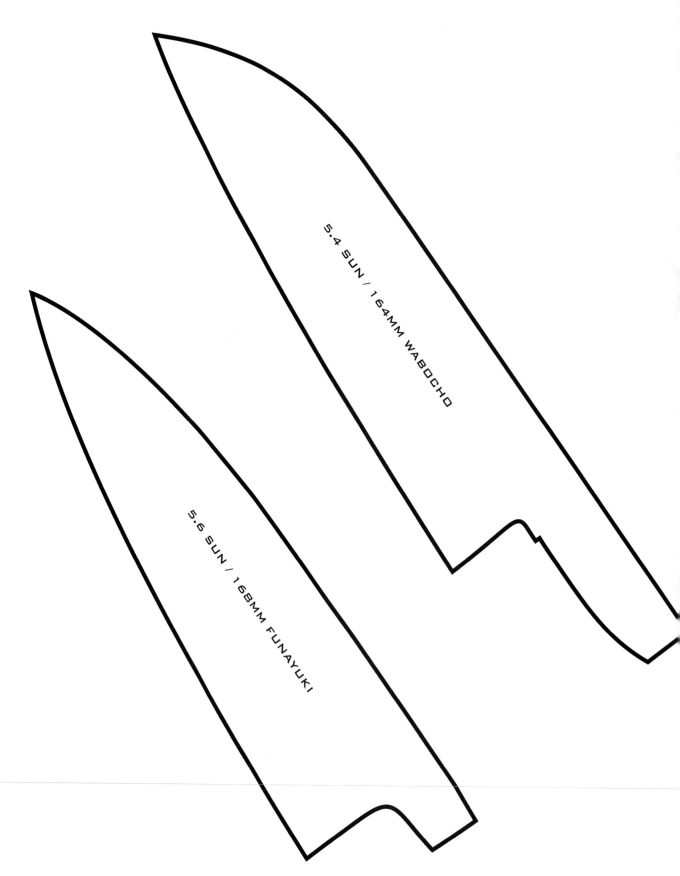

5.4 SUN / 164MM WABOCHO

5.6 SUN / 168MM FUNAYUKI

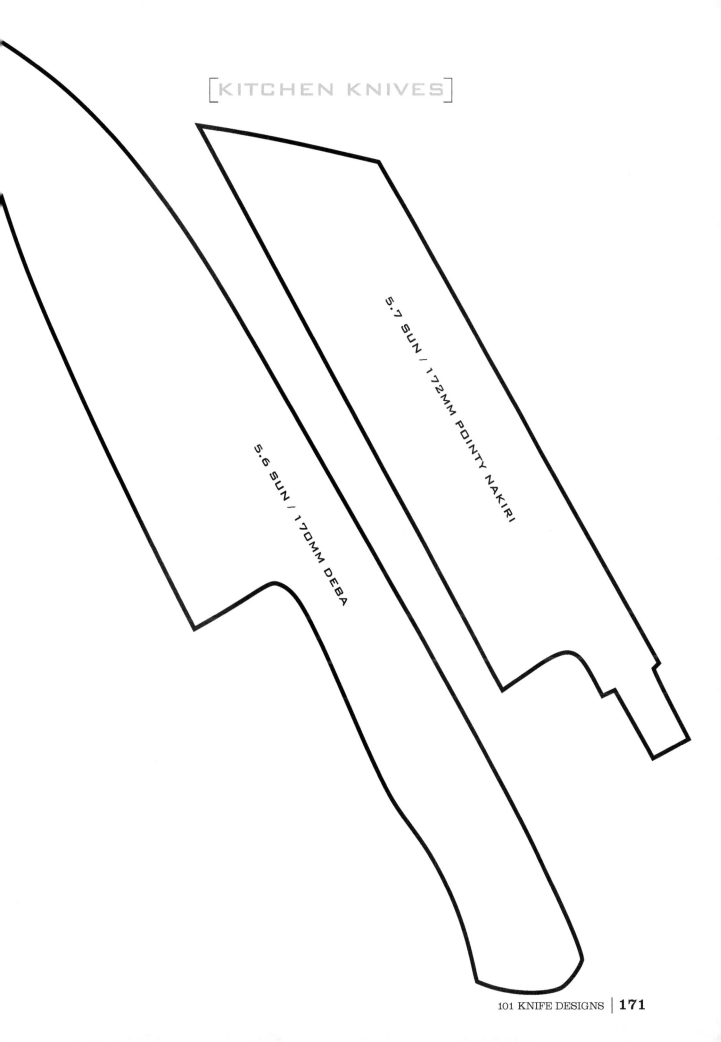

5.7 SUN / 172MM POINTY NAKIRI

5.6 SUN / 170MM DEBA

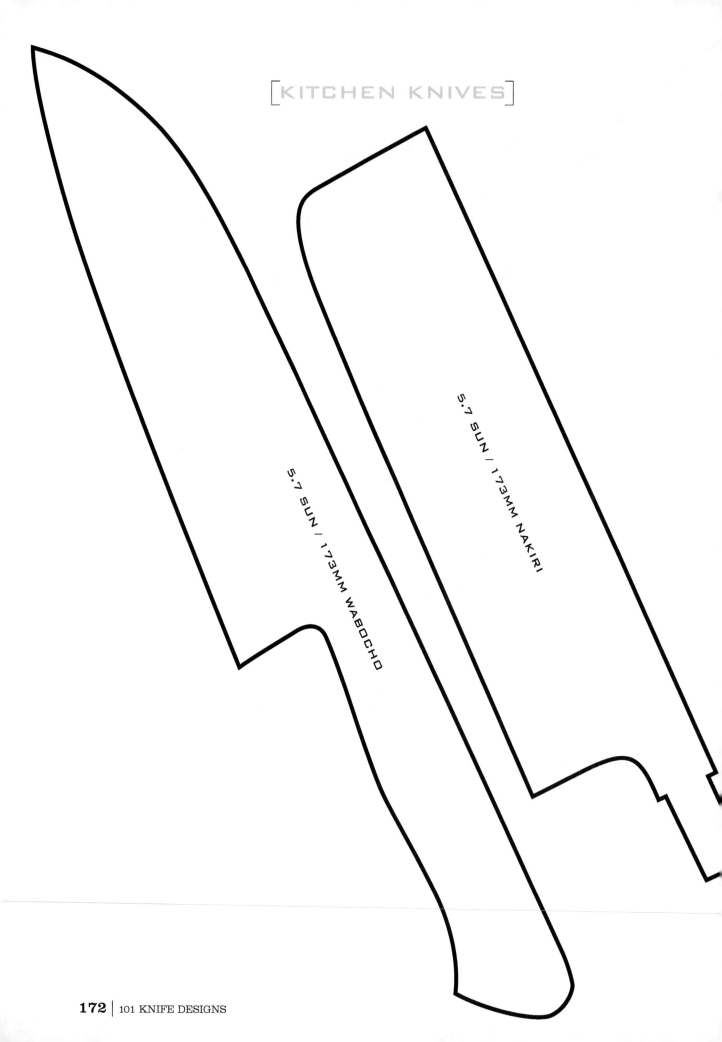

5.7 SUN / 173MM NAKIRI

5.7 SUN / 173MM WABOCHO

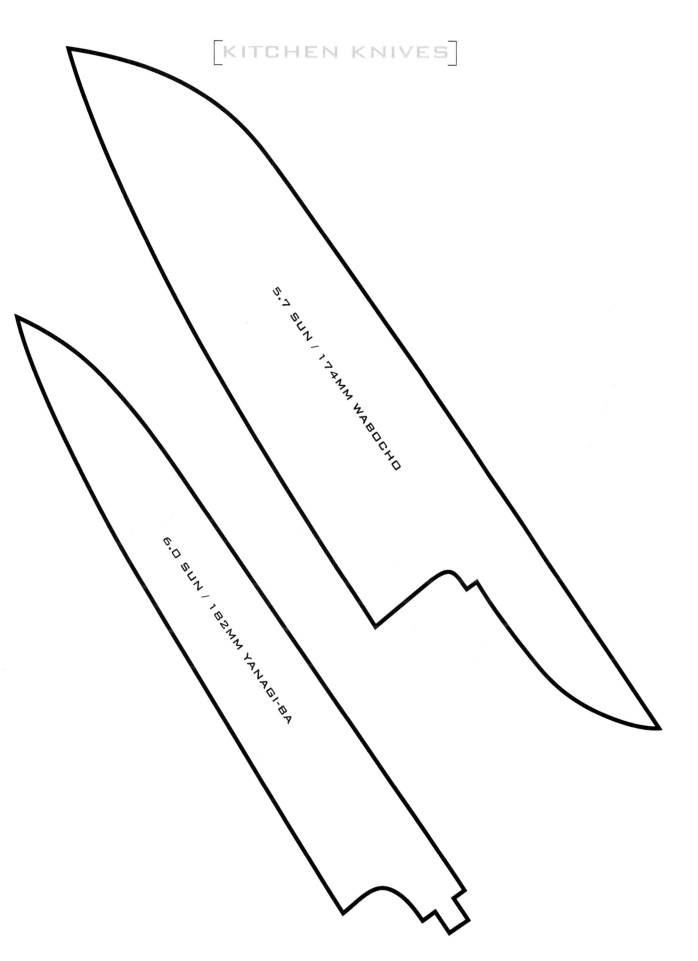

5.7 SUN / 174MM WABOCHO

6.0 SUN / 182MM YANAGI-BA

6.6 SUN / 200MM KIRITSUKI

6.2 SUN / 189MM NARROW FUNAYUKI

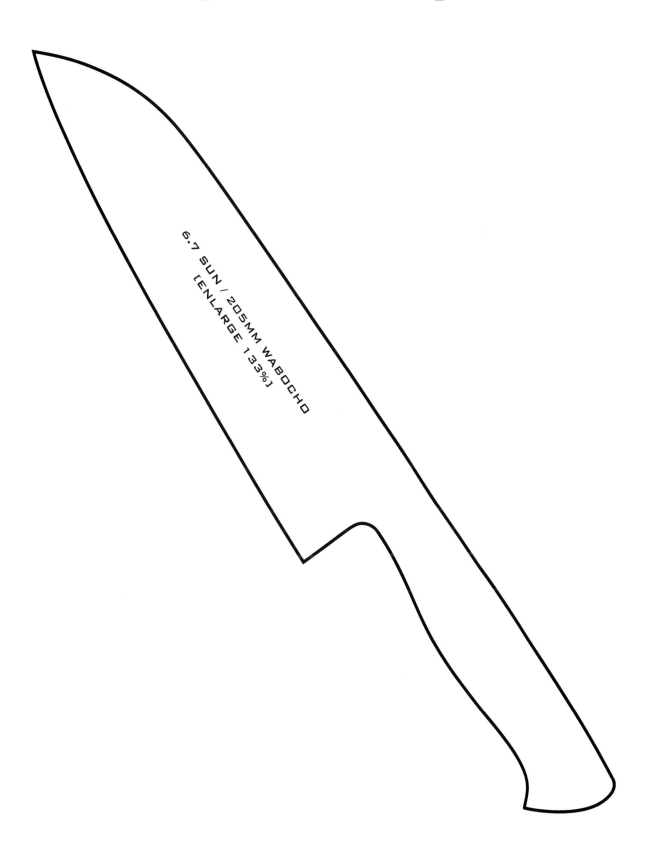

6.7 SUN / 205MM WABOCHO
[ENLARGE 133%]

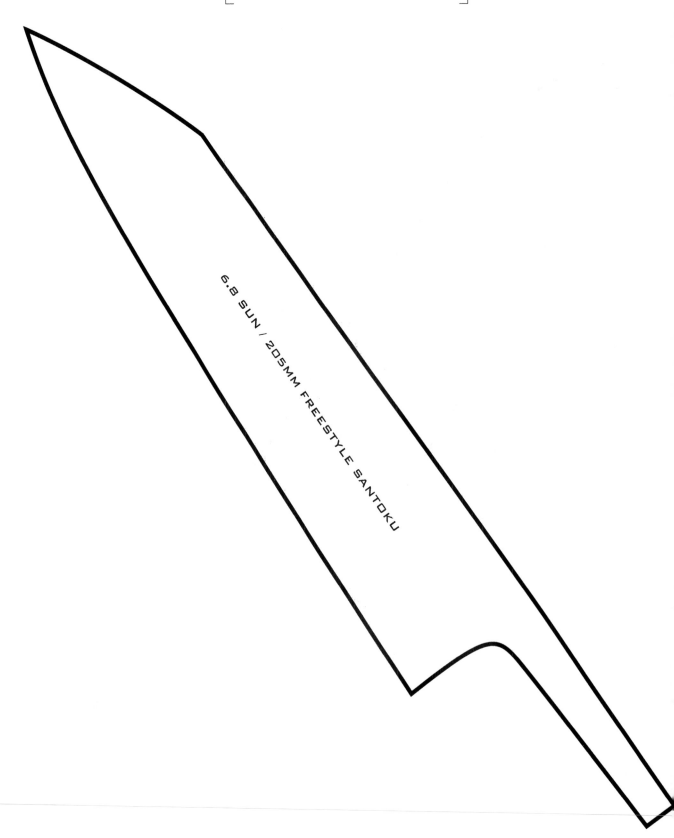

6.8 SUN / 205MM FREESTYLE SANTOKU

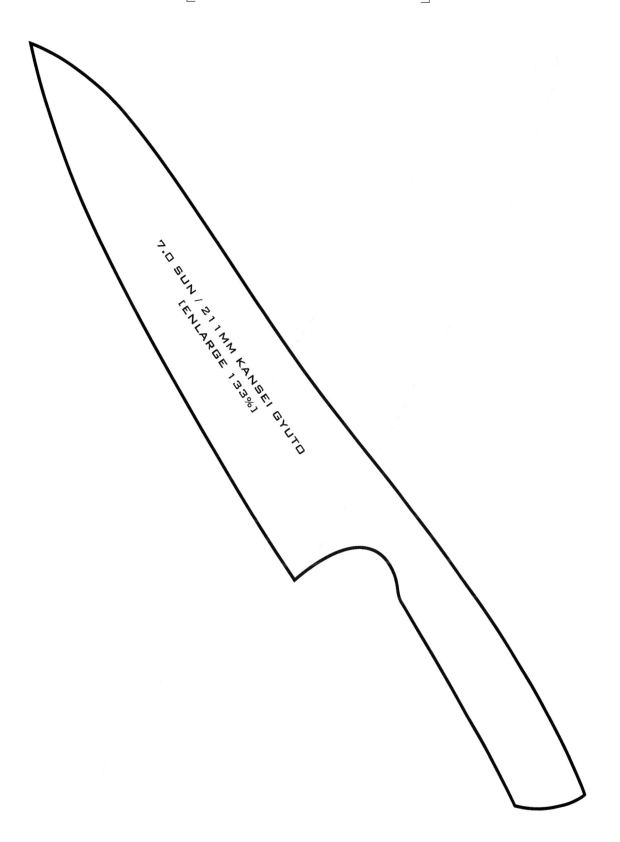

7.0 SUN / 211MM KANSEI GYUTO
[ENLARGE 133%]

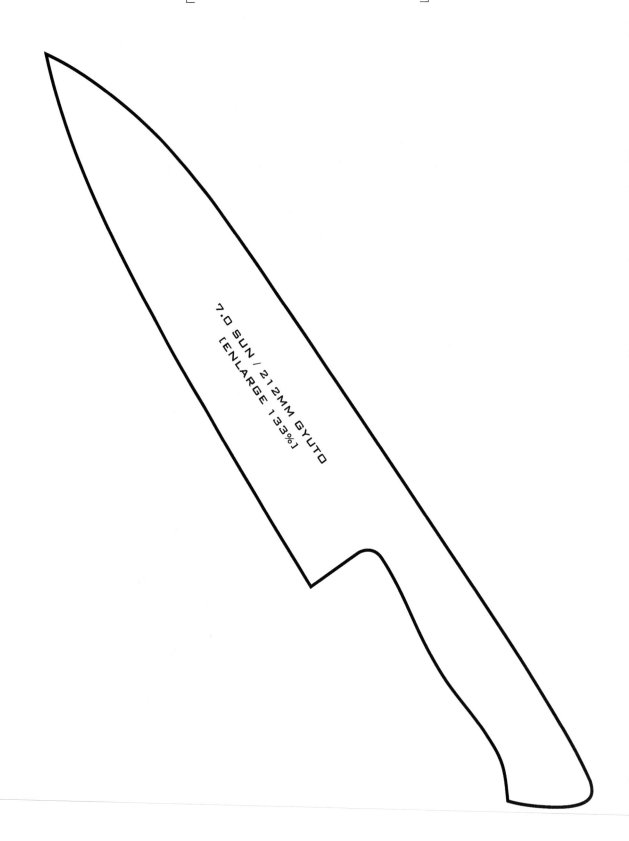

7.0 SUN / 212MM GYUTO
[ENLARGE 133%]

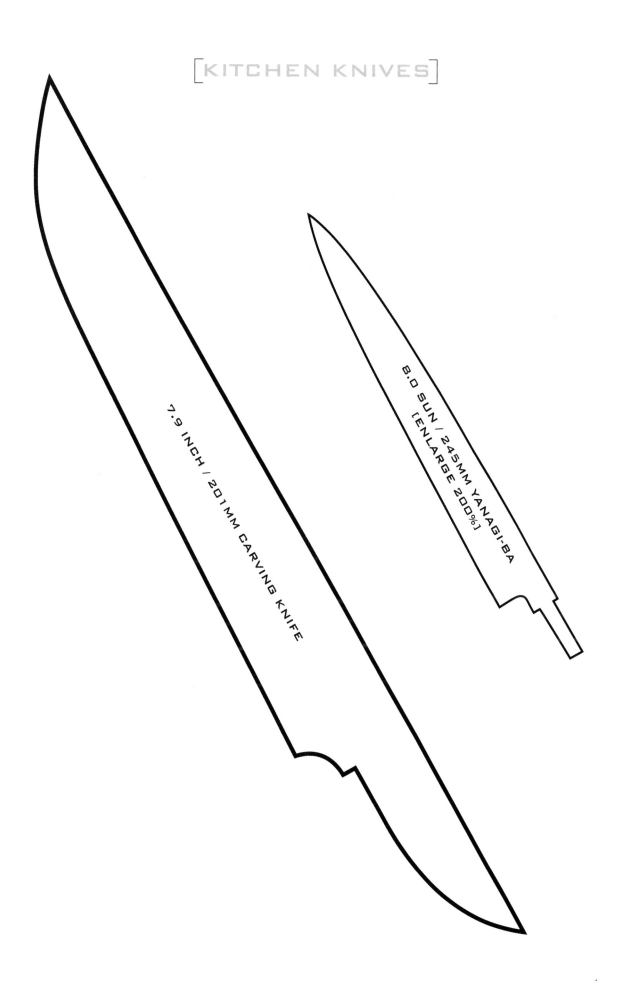

8.0 SUN / 245MM YANAGI-BA
[ENLARGE 200%]

7.9 INCH / 201MM CARVING KNIFE

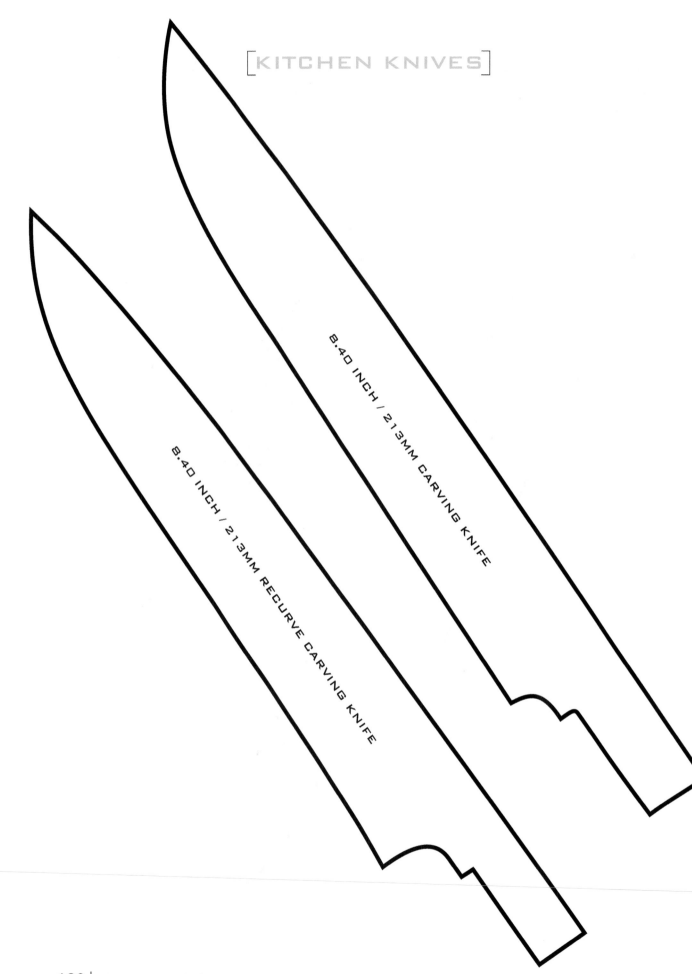

8.40 INCH / 213MM CARVING KNIFE

8.40 INCH / 213MM RECURVE CARVING KNIFE

9.6 SUN / 290MM GYUTO
[ENLARGE 200%]

10.0 SUN / 301MM GYUTO
[ENLARGE 200%]

12.3 SUN / 373MM GYUTO FUNAYUKI
[ENLARGE 200%]

10.2 SUN / 309MM YANAGI-BA
[ENLARGE 200%]

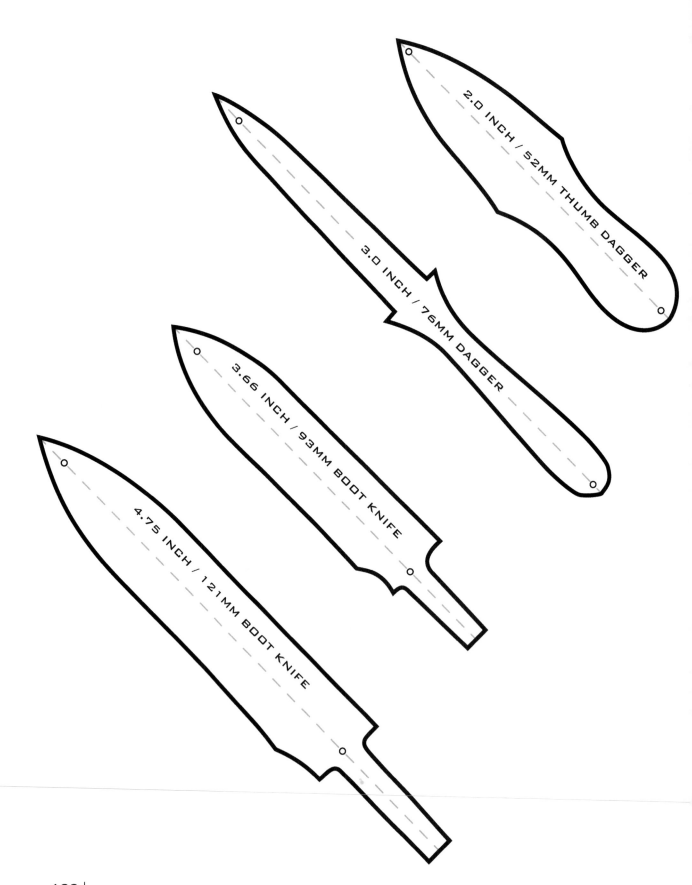

2.0 INCH / 52MM THUMB DAGGER

3.0 INCH / 76MM DAGGER

3.66 INCH / 93MM BOOT KNIFE

4.75 INCH / 121MM BOOT KNIFE

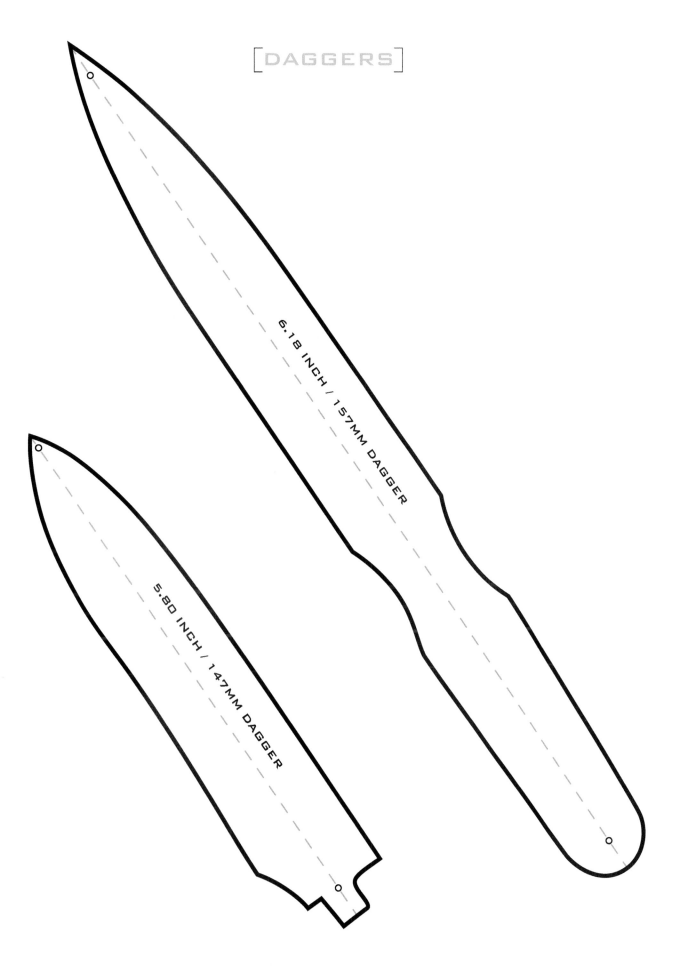

6.18 INCH / 157MM DAGGER

5.80 INCH / 147MM DAGGER

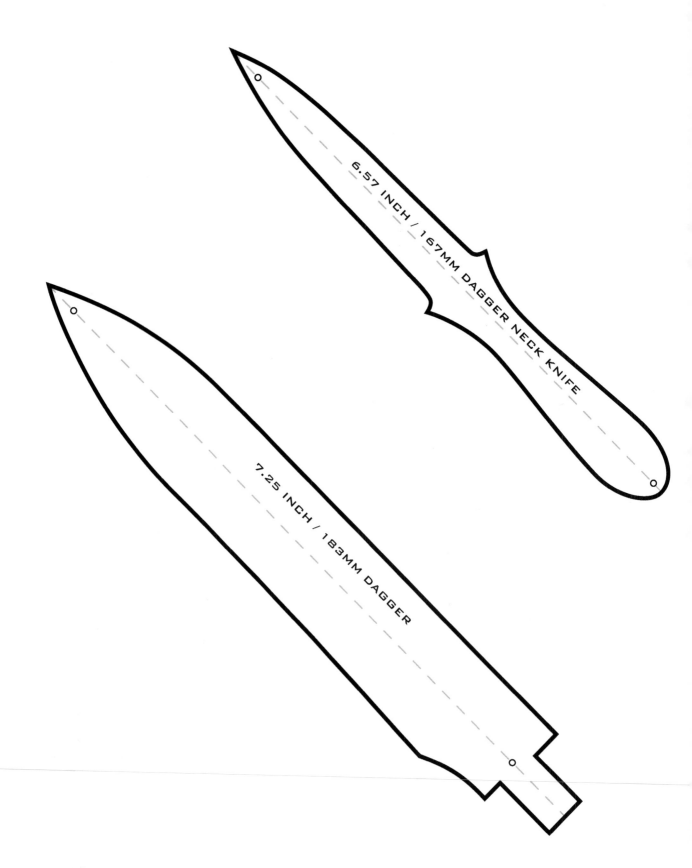

6.57 INCH / 167MM DAGGER NECK KNIFE

7.25 INCH / 183MM DAGGER

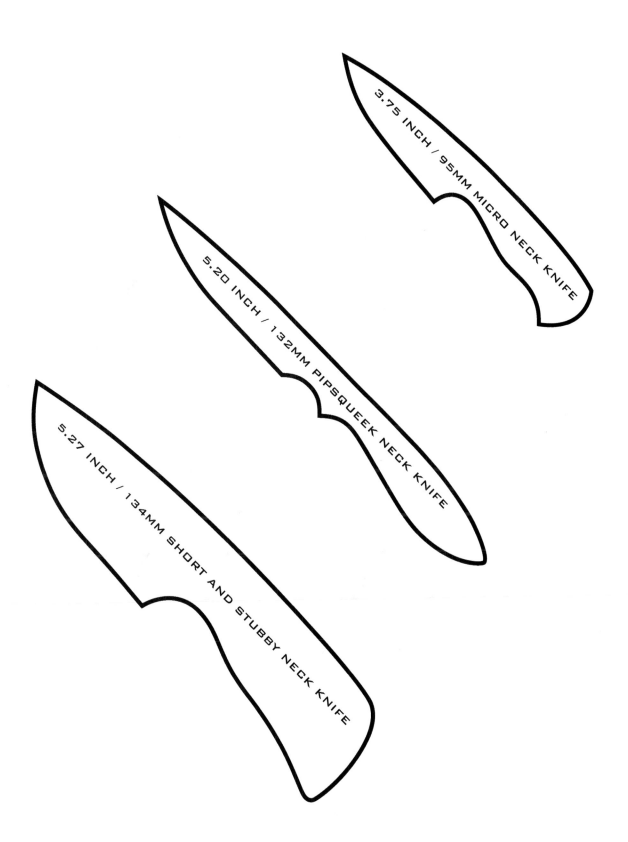

3.75 INCH / 95MM MICRO NECK KNIFE

5.20 INCH / 132MM PIPSQUEEK NECK KNIFE

5.27 INCH / 134MM SHORT AND STUBBY NECK KNIFE

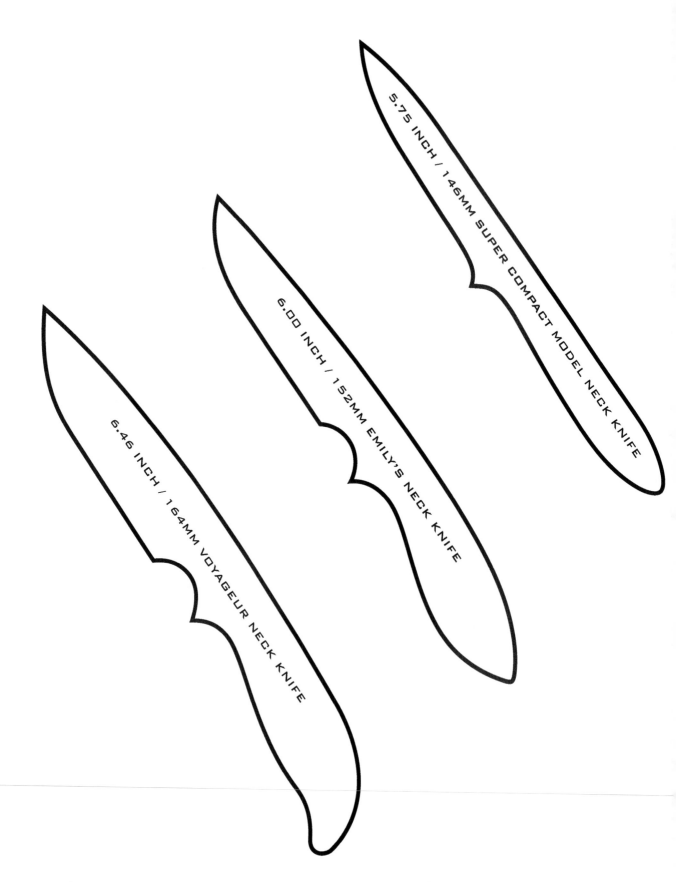

5.75 INCH / 146MM SUPER COMPACT MODEL NECK KNIFE

6.00 INCH / 152MM EMILY'S NECK KNIFE

6.46 INCH / 164MM VOYAGEUR NECK KNIFE

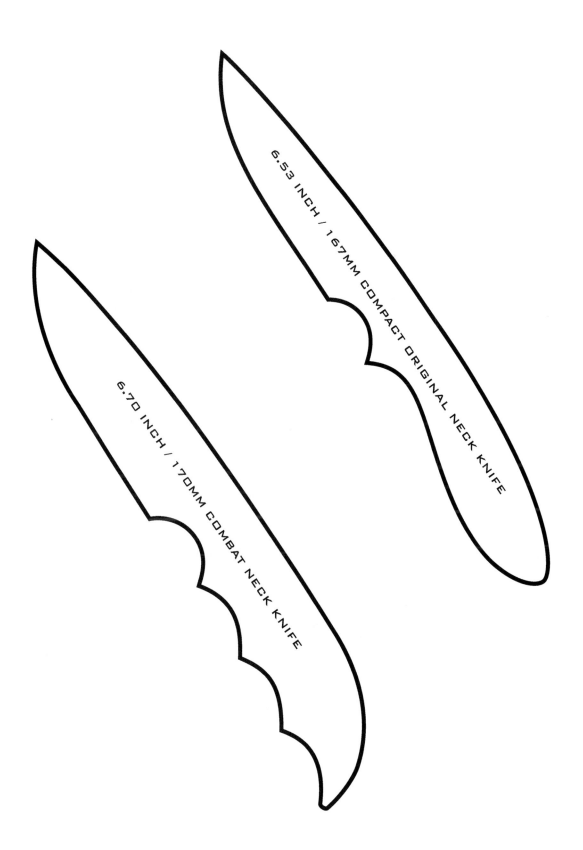

6.53 INCH / 167MM COMPACT ORIGINAL NECK KNIFE

6.70 INCH / 170MM COMBAT NECK KNIFE

6.89 INCH / 175MM TEKITO

7.00 INCH / 177MM HUMPBACK SKINNER NECK KNIFE

7.00 INCH / 177MM ORIGINAL MODEL NECK KNIFE

7.05 INCH / 179MM CLIP POINT ORIGINAL NECK KNIFE

7.13 INCH / 181MM BADLAND NECK KNIFE

7.17 INCH / 182MM WHARNCLIFFE NECK KNIFE

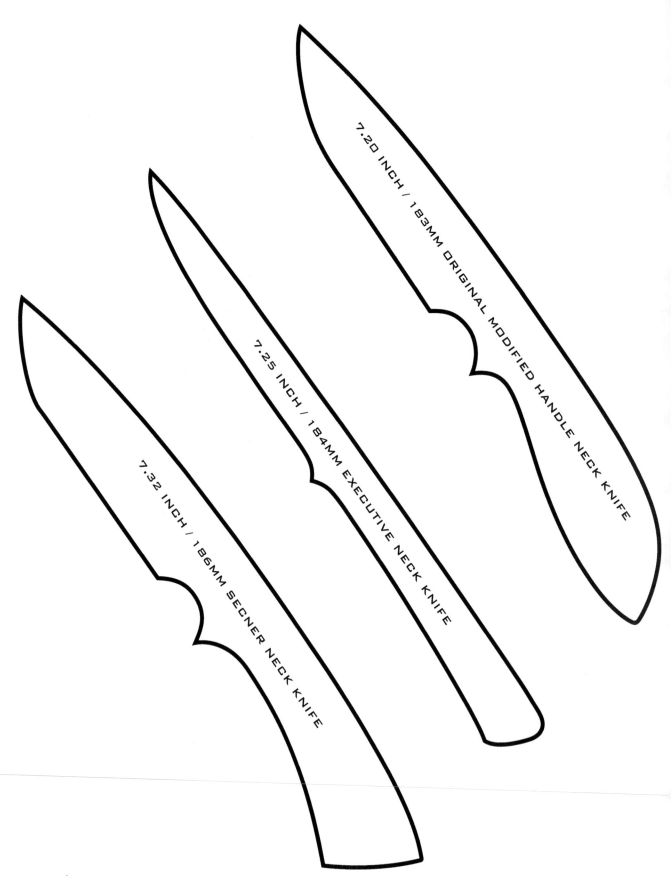

7.20 INCH / 183MM ORIGINAL MODIFIED HANDLE NECK KNIFE

7.25 INCH / 184MM EXECUTIVE NECK KNIFE

7.32 INCH / 186MM SECNER NECK KNIFE

7.32 INCH / 186MM TACTICAL NECK KNIFE

7.32 INCH / 186MM TACTICAL CLIP POINT NECK KNIFE

7.36 INCH / 187MM CLAVE NECK KNIFE

7.40 INCH / 188MM VEX CLIP NECK KNIFE

7.40 INCH / 188MM WHARNCLIFFE BRUTE NECK KNIFE

7.48 INCH / 190MM TETSUO'S NECK KNIFE

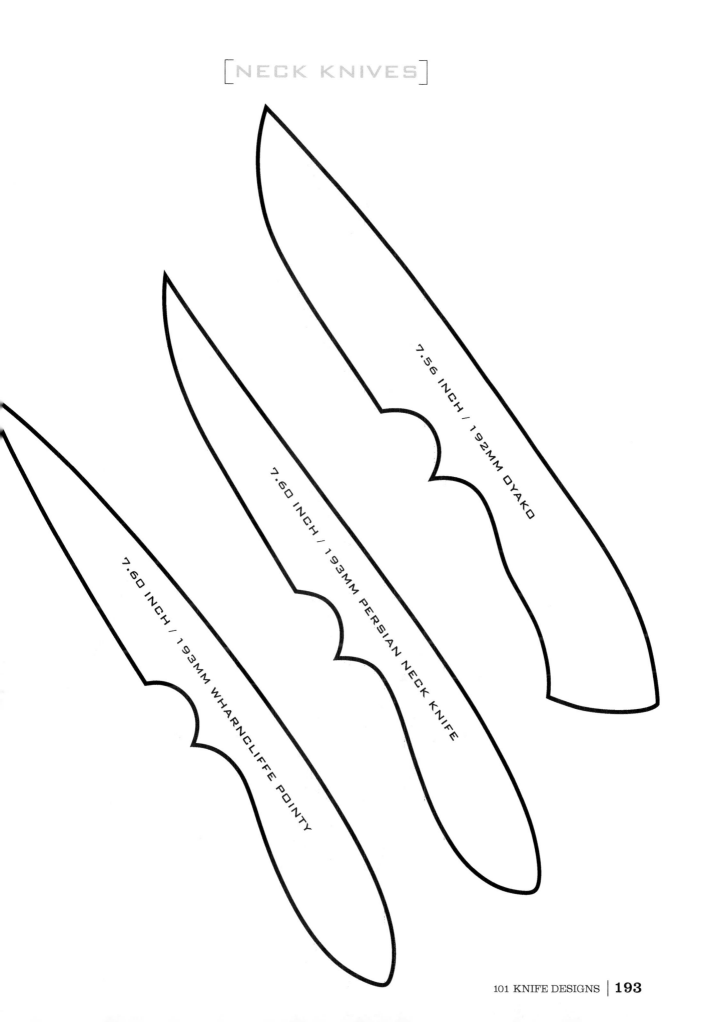

7.56 INCH / 192MM OYAKO

7.60 INCH / 193MM PERSIAN NECK KNIFE

7.60 INCH / 193MM WHARNCLIFFE POINTY

7.72 INCH / 196MM LONG & SLIM ORIGINAL NECK KNIFE

7.72 INCH / 196MM TACTICAL VEX CLIP NECK KNIFE

7.80 INCH / 198MM PERSIAN NECK KNIFE

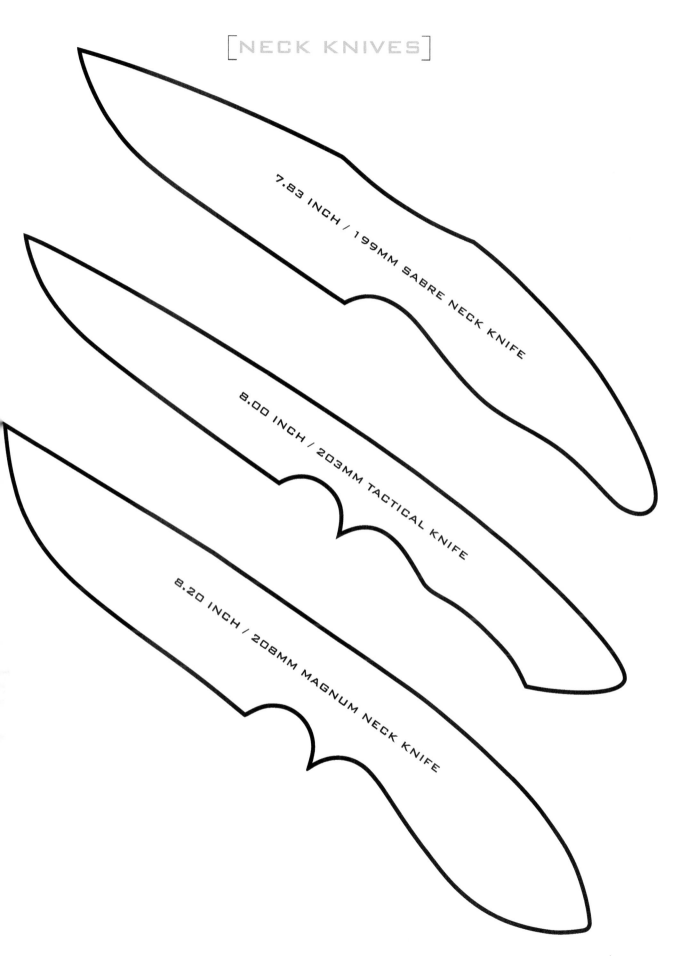

7.83 INCH / 199MM SABRE NECK KNIFE

8.00 INCH / 203MM TACTICAL KNIFE

8.20 INCH / 208MM MAGNUM NECK KNIFE

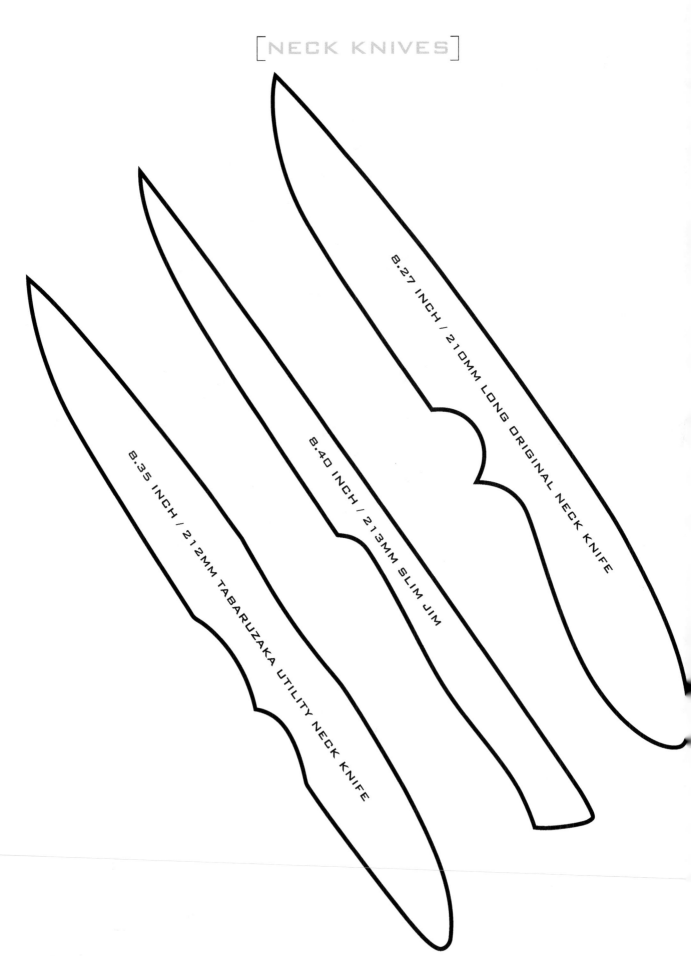

8.27 INCH / 210MM LONG ORIGINAL NECK KNIFE

8.40 INCH / 213MM SLIM JIM

8.35 INCH / 212MM TABARUZAKA UTILITY NECK KNIFE

5.6 SUN / 170MM KIRIDASHI

6.5 SUN / 199MM KIRIDASHI

6.1 SUN / 185MM KIRIDASHI

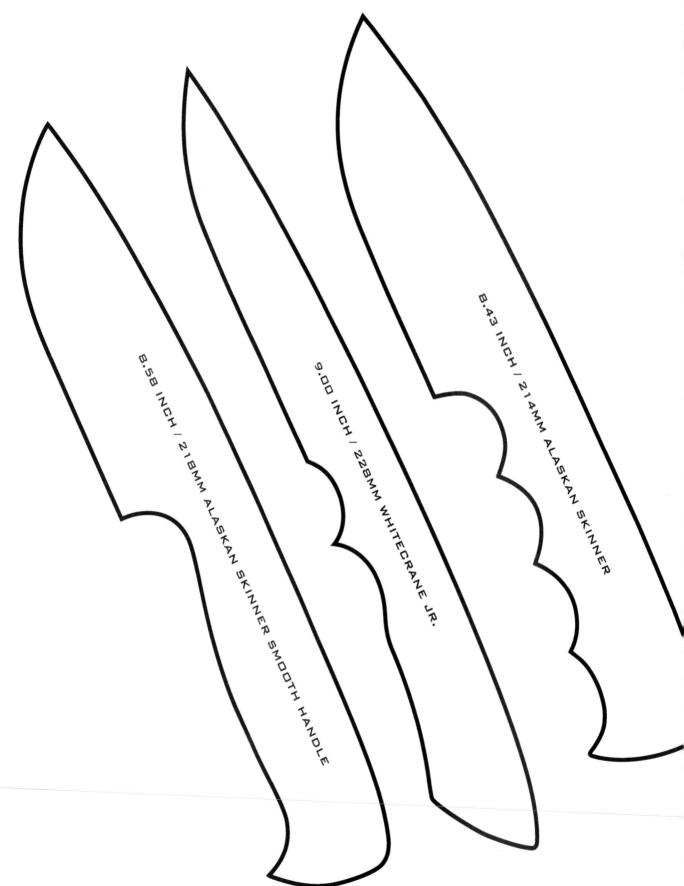

8.43 INCH / 214MM ALASKAN SKINNER

9.00 INCH / 228MM WHITECRANE JR.

8.58 INCH / 218MM ALASKAN SKINNER SMOOTH HANDLE

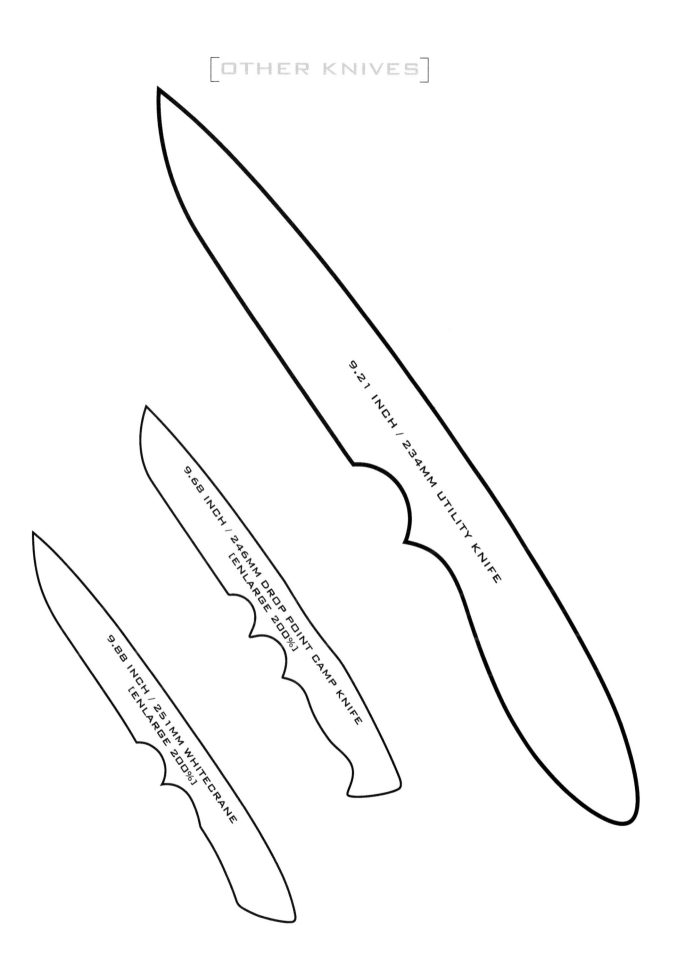

9.21 INCH / 234MM UTILITY KNIFE

9.68 INCH / 246MM DROP POINT CAMP KNIFE
[ENLARGE 200%]

9.88 INCH / 251MM WHITECRANE
[ENLARGE 200%]

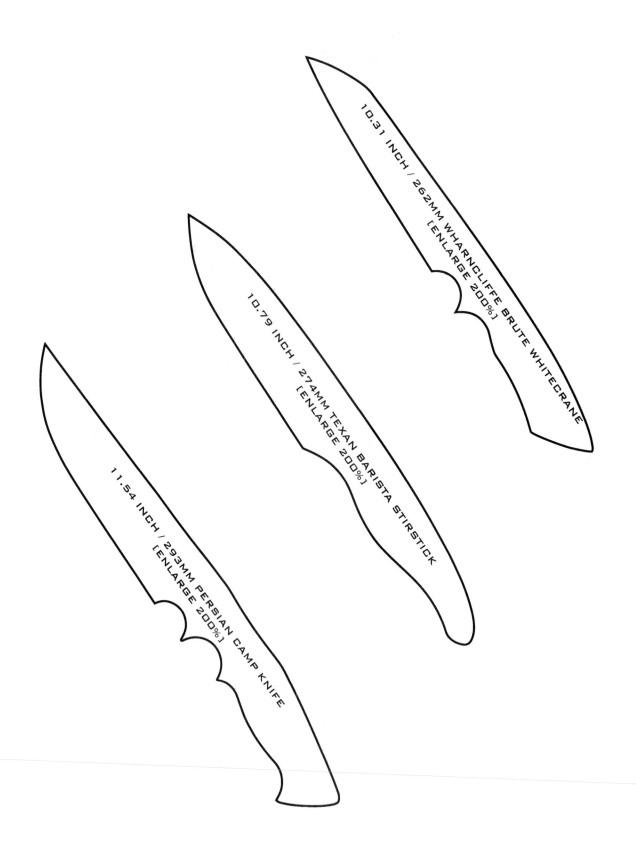

10.31 INCH / 262MM WHARNCLIFFE BRUTE WHITECRANE
[ENLARGE 200%]

10.79 INCH / 274MM TEXAN BARISTA STIRSTICK
[ENLARGE 200%]

11.54 INCH / 293MM PERSIAN CAMP KNIFE
[ENLARGE 200%]

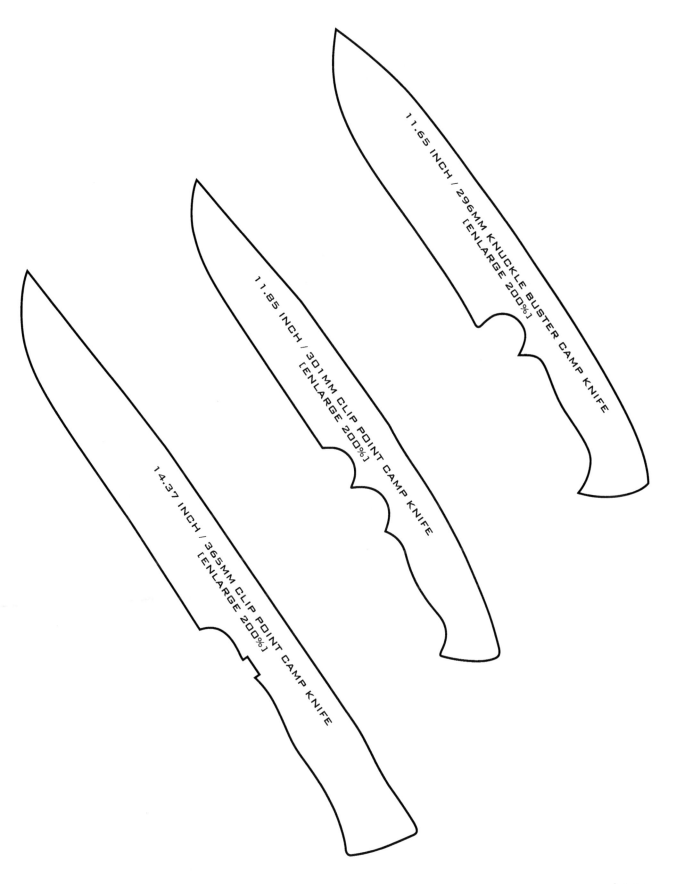

11.65 INCH / 296MM KNUCKLE BUSTER CAMP KNIFE
[ENLARGE 200%]

11.85 INCH / 301MM CLIP POINT CAMP KNIFE
[ENLARGE 200%]

14.37 INCH / 365MM CLIP POINT CAMP KNIFE
[ENLARGE 200%]

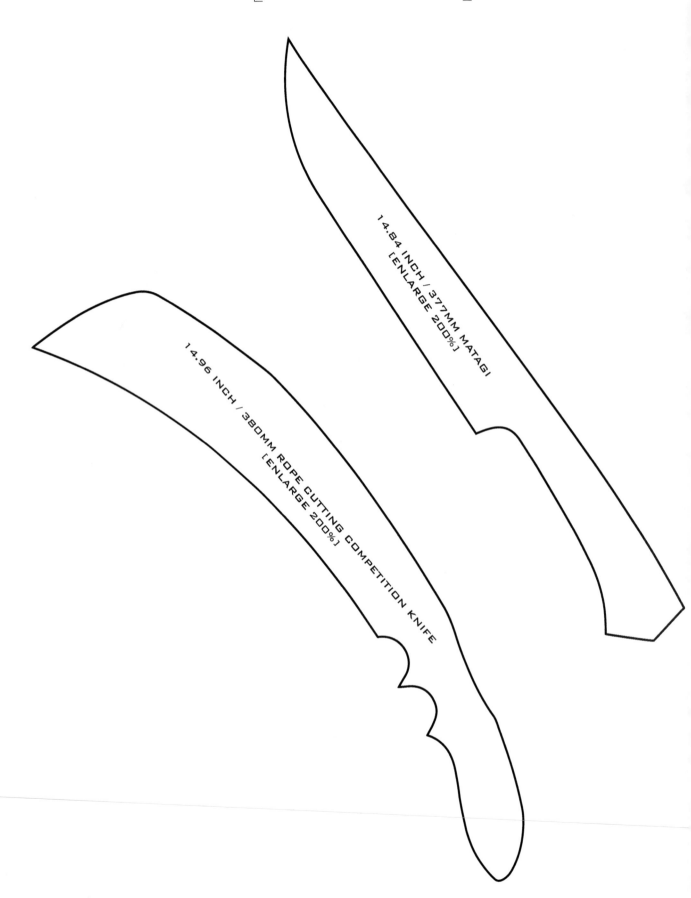

14.84 INCH / 377MM MATAGI
[ENLARGE 200%]

14.96 INCH / 380MM ROPE CUTTING COMPETITION KNIFE
[ENLARGE 200%]

15.75 INCH / 400MM RIO GRANDE CAMP KNIFE
[ENLARGE 200%]

20.83 INCH / 529MM STRAIGHT MACHETE
[ENLARGE 400%]

21.54 INCH / 547MM RECURVE MACHETE
[ENLARGE 400%]

[BIBLIOGRAPHY]

The following books were referenced during the writing of this book, not so much for the written text, but to study the shape and design of knives:

Burton, Richard F., *The Book of the Sword*, NY: Dover Publications, 1987

Edge, David and Paddock, John Miles, *Arms & Armor of the Medieval Knight,* NJ: Random House, 1996

Fowler, Ed, *Knife Talk, The Art & Science of Knifemaking*, WI: Krause Publications, 1998

Hart, Harold H., *Weapons & Armor; A Pictorial Archive of Woodcuts & Engravings*, NY: Dover Publications, 1978

Levine, Bernard R., *Levine's Guide To Knives and Their Values 2nd Edition*, IL: DBI Books, 1985

Levine, Bernard R., *Knifemakers of Old San Francisco*, CA: Badger Books, 1977

Mouret, Jean-Noel, *Knives of the World*, Surrey: Bramley Books, 1995

Walker, Greg, *Battle Blades; A Professional's Guide to Combat/Fighting Knives*, CO: Paladin Press, 1993

Tosa Hamono Catalog of Products, Tosa, Japan, 2000

ABOUT THE AUTHOR

When Murray isn't busy in the forge pounding on knives, teaching classes, guiding tours to Japan, filming educational videos, writing books, or practicing his husband and father skills, he likes to shoot guns, ride his BMW motorcycle, fly helicopters, fly planes and work out. In his free time he likes to relax.

For more information about the author's hand forged knives, exclusive bladesmithing classes, educational videos or the annual Carter Cutlery Japan Tour, please visit: www.cartercutlery.com

or contact Carter Cutlery directly at :

Carter Cutlery

2038 NW Aloclek Dr

Hillsboro OR 97124

503-466-1331

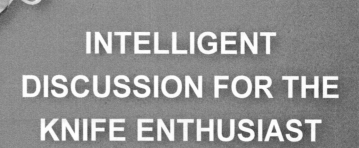